Apricot Jane bakes

Apricot Jane bakes

40 seasonal recipes to delight your palate

by

Jane Hatton

I am dedicating this book to the memory of my dear friend Gwen. We went to school together and became lifelong friends. We both loved to cook and bake – over 50 years of friendship, we shared meals, and family time, exchanged recipes and had such fun. Gwen would have loved to have shared this journey with me while I was writing this book. I feel blessed to have had a friend through all the changing scenes of life.

Thank you Gwen

Foreword

I have known Jane for many years as the most encouraging, inspiring, and patient bakery tutor. She has taken many aspiring bakers from novices to experts in her own inimitable way, gradually building up their skills, knowledge, and confidence until they can make their own unique marks in the wider baking industry. She has revelled in their success and commiserated with them over every failure, but always with a constructive suggestion about how they can improve. Bread, cake, and pastry lovers all over the country can taste the results of her efforts as these bakers are now plying their trade in the worldwide baking industry.

The fact that her renown has extended globally is entirely unsurprising to me. Jane's love of teaching is too big to be bounded by our shores, and I am so glad that she has been able to continue her teaching quest overseas.

I am even more glad that she has finally been able to write this lovely book, which draws together her baking wisdom and some truly mouth-watering recipes which are bold but simple enough for anyone to try.

With tips and hints to inspire every level of baker, and invaluable fault-finding information that will ensure success with every recipe, this book is a joyful leap into the world of the most delicious baking that should be on every baker's bookshelf.

Congratulations, Apricot Jane, this is a masterpiece!

Sara Autton BSc (Hons)
June 2022

*Sara has been in the baking industry all her working life
and is as passionate about passing on her knowledge.*

Contents

SPRING   55

Introduction

This book reflects recipes and problem-solving methods drawn from over 40 years of teaching bakery, confectionery, and sugarcraft.

Tailoring or Catering?

The secondary school I went to was a trade school in Kensington. I was able to choose my trade options at age 15 – a choice between Catering, Art, and Tailoring. I originally had Tailoring in mind, but this changed when I started watching what was happening in the school kitchen during lunch. The kitchen was bustling during lunch service. The professional cookers and beautiful copper pots captivated me. Somehow Tailoring didn't quite match up to that. My first City and Guilds qualification was in Catering. Very early on, I was introduced to competitions at Hotelympia, a hotel and restaurant show. Here, Salon Culinaire holds competitions for craft skills, and it was there that I won my first gold medal for my pastries at the age of 16. I would never have believed then that I would one day be Vice Chairman of Confectionery Judges at The Salon!

My first job was as a pastry chef. In the evenings, I studied bakery, followed by cake decoration. I became involved in the Bakery Students' Society, now called the Alliance of Bakery Students and Trainees (ABST), of which I am still a member. It is where I served as a competition secretary for over 10 years and as president. Currently, I am a judge in Confectionery. The ABST is a great platform to train young bakers for the industry!

Thanks to my amazing tutors

I owe so much to my tutors Jackie Cottrell from school and Alan Littlewood from college. They saw potential in me, guided me in the right direction, and helped me see that the baking industry was for me – a decision I would never regret. Inspired by them, I found work in a family bakery as a confectioner and head cake decorator.

In the evenings, I taught cake decoration in the local education centre. One day I was asked to cover a tutor's absence at the college – what an opportunity this proved to be! This led to a teaching qualification, and when a full-time job opened up, I embraced the change. The great thing was being able to teach in the industry I loved.

I think back to my first baking experience. I was stuck at home because I could not go to school as I was getting over tonsillitis, so I decided to make some cupcakes. While I was putting the creamed sugar, butter, and eggs into the cases and placing them in the oven, my dad said to me, "Don't you need some flour?" "Oh, no I don't" I replied, "Mum never puts flour in." You can imagine the sticky toffee mess!

You thought that was bad. Now picture this scene. I had been up since 5am, worked my socks off all day in the bakery, and now had an evening class in college. Having made my dough, I was waiting for it to prove, sitting at my table listening (or should I say trying to listen) to the evening lecture. Well, my eyes grew heavy and gently closed! The lecturer asked, "Can someone name a cereal?" I snapped out of my slumber, up went my hand in complete confidence, of course, and I said, 'Cornflakes!' I am glad to say I now understand flour! What can I say – we all have to start somewhere?

Teaching and baking go hand in hand

I must say that working in the industry and teaching at the same time gave me great experience. Understanding how to work with speed and to a specific standard meant I was able to incorporate my training into the workplace. I was involved with the local Association of Master Bakers, which enabled me to keep in touch with industry changes. It's so important when teaching to be up-to-date with current changes.

Training has been a delight, helping people to learn new skills and being involved with national competitions where we won many gold medals. My time at Brooklands College in Weybridge opened opportunities and invitations to Japan, Singapore, Hong Kong, Switzerland, and Ireland to teach sugarcraft techniques.

Bakery Training Award 2008

I received an invitation to apply for the Bakery Training Award in May 2008. At first, I put the letter to one side – after all, I was busy getting my students ready to compete, so I really didn't have time. I have my good friend Sue Haskell to thank for telling me to go for it. So, I had to put a portfolio together of my journey in training along with references from the industry and past students to show what impact I had on them through training. It still amazes me that in 2008 at the Grosvenor Hotel in London, I won the Bakery Training Award at the British Baking Awards, and what a privilege this was. This honour would lead me to new pastures.

I went back into the industry part-time as the Bakery Trainer for Cooplands, a family business based in Scarborough, Durham, and Hull. In Hull, I delivered courses to employees to develop their technical knowledge and problem-solving skills. Alongside this, I was working at the National Bakery School (NBS) within the London South Bank University, teaching Confectionery. This all led to me receiving the Freedom of the City of London and becoming Liveryman to the Worshipful Company of Bakers.

So why call this book Apricot Jane Bakes?

I have my students at the NBS to blame for this – they nick-named me 'Apricot Jane.' In the bakery, we use apricot jam quite a bit for glazing and finishing. I could have been called something a lot worse! On reflection, I have always been drawn to apricots. As a student, apricot was my go-to colour in cake decoration, and when I got married, my bridesmaids were in apricot, so it seemed fitting.

I have laid out this book in seasons: spring, summer, autumn, and winter. And this is where you will find the recipes, hints, and tips. Preceding the recipes, you will find technical information on methods and ingredient functions together with fault-finding charts. It would be beneficial to read through these sections to develop your understanding of the materials and methods used and avoid some of the trips along the way. Bakery requires continual evaluation in problem solving, and it doesn't matter how long you have been baking. There will always be a challenge.

I wanted to give back to others the gifts and skills I have learned over 40 years of baking and teaching bakery. Life is a journey with twists and turns. We need strength for each day which I have found in my Christian faith: "Taste and see that the Lord is good," Psalm 34:8. Sharing my experience will hopefully inspire you to bake, understand the functions of ingredients, be able to problem solve, and deliver a successful quality product.

My motto has been "Quality is delighting the customer."

So, have fun and enjoy baking!

Apricot Jane

Ingredient Functions

It is important to understand the roles and functions of each ingredient used in baking. It doesn't matter how long you have been baking; we always need to evaluate and assess the product to be able to identify what went wrong and find a solution.

So, let's look at the ingredients we will be using under each heading:

Flour

This is the main ingredient in most recipes, so it is important to know which flour to use for each product and understand the reasons why.

Flour is made from cereal grains, mostly wheat. Basically, the wheat grain has three main parts, the bran, the endosperm, and the germ.

The outer protective covering of the wheat grain is called the **bran** – this is high in fibre and nutritious with vitamins and minerals. It softens in water and is capable of absorbing moisture.

The inside of the wheat grain is the endosperm which is the starch, and this has the two main proteins, glutenin and gliadin. When wetted and developed by kneading, they create a network called the gluten network. The gluten network has a key role in breadmaking as it creates an elastic network that traps the gas produced by fermenting the yeast, creating volume and structure in the bread. The percentage of gluten-forming proteins in flour is important to understand when choosing flour for a product.

The **germ** is a very small part of the wheat grain and is rich in fat, vitamins, and minerals. Also, the germ has vital enzymes which break down the endosperm (starch) to provide food for the yeast. The germ is the embryo and, given the correct conditions, can germinate and create a new plant.

The function of flour is to give structure and texture to the bread, cake, pastry, and biscuits, and this will vary according to the flour used and the product made.

The flours I have used in my recipes are all available in the supermarkets.

Strong flour has a higher percentage of protein content, around 14%, which can be developed to create elasticity in the dough. White strong flour has the bran and germ removed.

Whole wheat flour has the whole grain (bran, endosperm, and germ), often referred to as wholemeal flour. It can be stone ground (this is crushing the grain between two granite millstones) which gives a nuttier flavour and is a little coarser than roller-milled flour. Wholemeal flour will require more liquid as the bran is a thirsty ingredient.

Semolina flour is made from Durham wheat and is high in protein.

Rye flour – although rye flour has enough gliadin, it is low in glutenin, so the gluten development is low, resulting in the volume and texture of bread having a closer crumb structure.

Whole grain and seeded flour are usually a wholemeal base, with the addition of grains and/or seeds to give a lovely texture and flavour. You can buy granary flour, country grain, or mixed grain flour.

Plain flour has a lower gluten protein which is between 9-11.5%, but this can vary with different brands. This flour is suitable for cakes, pastries, and biscuits.

Self-raising flour is plain flour with raising agents added (baking powder) and is used for quickness. It is not suitable for bread making, but good for cakes and biscuits.

Cornflour is processed from maize. It is a starch and has no gluten. It is used for thickening and particularly in cakes and muffins.

Spelt flour is like wheat. It has a slightly nutty flavour and contains gluten.

Storage conditions for flours are pretty much the same. They need to be in cool, dry sealed containers away from moisture as this will encourage mould growth.

Aerating ingredients

Baking powder is a chemical raising agent. It contains one-part alkali (bicarbonate of soda) and two parts acid (cream of tartar). Baking powder is used to aerate products and creates carbon dioxide gas, which helps tenderize the crumb structure, creates volume, and contributes to the cell size of the crumb.

A small amount of bicarbonate of soda in chocolate cakes and gingerbreads provides a darker crumb colour and texture. In cookies, it will contribute to the flow by opening the cookie and help the product become crisp with a good colour (see gingerbread biscuits).

Sugar

Sugar comes from sugar beet or sugar cane which is plant based. It is refined for use in baking by extracting the juice by washing, clarifying, and filtering the syrups before crystallizing into the various sugar types. Sugar is hygroscopic, which means it absorbs moisture. Sugars, therefore, need to be kept in airtight containers to stop them from going hard, especially brown sugar.

This reminds me of my early days of teaching. I ordered a 25kg bag of dark soft brown sugar to cover my Christmas classes for Christmas cakes. I kept the sugar sealed in the bag. When it came to using the sugar for simnel cakes for my Easter classes, the sugar had become a rock!

A lesson learned: store in an airtight container.

Granulated sugar used in some biscuit baked goods it is coarse in texture.

Caster sugar – used in cakes, pastry, meringues, and bread. It has a fine grain.

Golden caster sugar used in cakes has more flavour and is light gold in colour.

Demerara sugar is golden in colour and is like granulated sugar. It is used for toppings and coffee.

Soft brown sugar contains about 6% molasses. It is a soft, moist sugar, has a good flavour and it can hold moisture.

Dark brown sugars come from raw cane. They are soft and moist and give good flavour because of the 18% molasses, which gives colour to the cake crumb – used a lot in rich fruit cakes.

Icing sugar is white, very finely milled, used for dusting, and as an ingredient for some pastries and royal icing for cake decorating and ready-to-roll sugar paste.

Functions of sugar

During the mixing process, sugar acts as a tenderizing agent by absorbing water and slowing gluten development.

It aerates cake batters in the creaming process, promoting volume and lightness.

Sugar sweetens and enriches products and adds flavour and colour depending on the sugar type. Sugar helps to promote spread in cookies and helps with the crust and crispiness of baked goods.

Maillard reaction

At high temperatures, sugar chemically reacts with protein in the baking products, contributing to their browned surface.

The Maillard reaction is named after the French chemist, L. C. Maillard, who first explained how it happens. It is a complex chemical reaction between sugars, amino acids, peptides, and other proteins in baking products, causing the surfaces to turn brown. It is the same reaction that causes bread slices to turn brown in a toaster.

During the baking of breads, Maillard reactions occur among sugar and the amino acids, peptides, or proteins from other ingredients in the baked products, causing the browning.

These reactions contribute to the aroma associated with the baked goods. The higher the sugar content of the baked good, the darker golden brown the surface appears. As described above, these browned surfaces not only taste good but help retain moisture in the baked product, prolonging its freshness.

Syrups

Syrups help sweeten, moisten and brown baked goods and so must be carefully balanced in a recipe.

Golden syrup is a thick amber-coloured invert syrup containing water and citric acid, used in cakes using a hot method as the syrup is heavy. It is also used in biscuits.

Treacle is darker in colour and used to enhance the cake crumb colour in rich fruit cakes, and it helps to keep moisture in a cake.

Glucose is another invert sugar used to prevent the crystallization of sugar in ice creams, caramels, and sugar required for pulling and making flowers. It can be used as an ingredient in sugar pastes.

Honey is a natural invert sugar and gives a lovely flavour. The flavour varies according to where the bees pollinate the flowers. It can be added to cakes and biscuits and some enriched goods.

Eggs

Eggs are an important ingredient. They can be used whole or separated where the egg yolk and egg white have different functions.

Eggs contain 74% water, so adding an egg to a batter or a dough means moisture is added. When eggs are whisked, they can increase in volume by incorporating air. Eggs can aerate their own weight in flour.

Sometimes called Albumen, egg white is the protein of egg. A stiff foam can be made from the albumen with sugar, thus forming a meringue. Albumen has no flavour.

Egg yolks contain a natural emulsifier called lecithin, which helps to provide stability to the mixture as it will help hold fat and liquid together.

As heat is applied during baking, the air in the foam expands to provide aeration to the baked cake.

Eggs provide structure to the cake. When subjected to heat, the bubbles in the aerated mixture expand until the egg coagulates, which establishes the structure.

Eggs provide flavour and colour, and free-range eggs especially are rich in both. Eggs are high in protein and fat, making them a highly nutritious ingredient.

Many products, e.g., some breads, pastries, and scones, benefit from a pre-bake glaze, which is done by brushing with whole egg, yolk, or whites. This enhances the product by giving it a shiny surface.

An egg's moistening, emulsifying and enriching properties help prolong a product's shelf life.

You will notice that, in most recipes, eggs need to be weighed to help your accuracy. An average egg weighs 50g, with the yolk being about 20g and the white about 30g. Accuracy helps to get a quality product. Use eggs at room temperature for the best results.

Whenever I talk about eggs in recipes, I can't help but smile when I remember a student whom I had asked to separate five eggs ready for the next stage of the process. I moved around the class to each group, arriving back to the student separating five eggs to find that there was a group of two eggs and a group of three eggs instead of five yolks and five whites. On clarifying what I wanted, the response was, "I didn't know that you could do that."

Never assume everyone knows what you mean.

Fats

Butter

Butter is a dairy product and is available in salted and unsalted forms. Butter is made from souring or ripened cream and has excellent creaming properties for cake making. The flavours will vary depending on what type of butter you buy. For best results, do not use light butter where water content is high and fat content low.

Shortening

Shortening was originally developed as a replacement for lard, an animal fat. It is 100% fat and contains no water. It is white and has good creaming properties. There is no flavour, and I sometimes use a small percentage of shortening in cakes as it helps to soften the crumb, open the structure, and increase volume.

Cake margarine

Cake margarine can be used in place of butter. It is cheaper but lacks the flavour of butter. Cake margarine has good creaming properties and is available unsalted and salted.

Vegetable oil

Vegetable oil contains no water and is 100% fat. When used in a cake, it helps to give a light soft texture with a tender crumb that is moist. Olive oil is heavier and works well in some breads, such as focaccia and pizzas. It helps to give an open crumb structure. Sunflower and vegetable oils are best for cakes and muffins.

Fresh dairy cream

Fresh dairy cream is obtained from the fat of the milk. The type of cream (single, double, or whipping) is indicated by the percentage of fat content.

Fresh dairy cream must always be stored in a refrigerator at 4°C to ensure that it is safe to eat. In the baking industry, it is classified as a high-risk ingredient, and everyone who uses it is aware that it must be stored correctly and used as fresh as possible.

Single cream has an 18% butterfat content. Single cream is best used for sauces and pouring. It can't be whipped.

Whipping cream has a 35-37% butterfat content. Whipping cream, as the name suggests, can be whipped, used as a filling, coating, and for piping.

Double cream has a 48% butterfat content. Double cream can be whipped and used for rich fillings, mousses, coatings, and ganache. If double cream is over whipped the fat globules pull together, and butter can be made.

Clotted cream has a minimum of 55% butterfat content. Clotted cream can't be whipped. It is used to top scones or for quenelles for deserts.

Additives

Additives are used to help keep the cream stable. For example, sugar (up to 13%) is one such additive, and it also adds flavour.

Gelatine may be used to set cream for mousse-type fillings up to 0.3%.

Milk

Milk can be used as an ingredient in cakes and bread, and full-fat milk is best. Milk helps to enrich the product, tenderise the crumb, extend shelf life, help with crust colour, as well as add flavour to the products.

Yeast

Yeast is part of the fungus family and is used to aerate bread. Yeast produces carbon dioxide gas and ethyl alcohol to create a light sponge-like texture. Yeast feeds on sugars which enable fermentation. It is temperature sensitive and works best at 26°C (a little above room temperature). Yeast provides flavour through the complex production of alcohol and organic acids, which are by-products of its fermentation.

Salt helps to control the rate of fermentation but, in excess, has a retarding (slowing down) effect on yeast activity. High levels of fat and spices can also have retarding effects on yeast. You will notice that in enriched bread doughs, the yeast amount is higher to compensate for the retarding effect. Yeast can be bought fresh or dried. Most of my recipes are based on dried yeast. Sachets normally hold 7g of dried yeast, but always check the packet. You may need to calculate the amount of yeast required, depending on whether you are using fresh or dried.

Divide the amount by 3 to convert from fresh to dried (for example, 30g fresh yeast divided by 3 = 10g dried yeast).

Alternatively, take dried yeast and multiply by 3 to convert it to fresh yeast (7g dried yeast equates to: 7g x 3 = 21g of fresh yeast).

Salt

Salt is a natural mineral that gives flavour and adds to the eating quality of the product, whether sweet or savoury. It improves crust colour, controls fermentation, and increases shelf life. It also helps to develop the gluten structure in bread.

Fruit

Candied and dried fruits (such as sultanas, currants, raisins, candied peel, cherries, and apricots) all add flavour, moisture, and texture to cakes. Fruits can be puréed and frozen as well as used fresh.

Nuts

Nuts add texture, flavour, moisture, and colour to cakes and pastries. They should be used fresh and kept in a cold dark place. The most popular are almonds used whole, nibbled (lightly chopped), or ground, and hazel nuts used whole and ground. Walnuts are often used in pieces or walnut halves and used for decoration. Pistachios have become popular due to their lovely green colour. For best results, coconut should be dried and desiccated before use.

Marzipan

This is a product made from almonds. It may be used as an ingredient, moulded, and used as a covering.

Chocolate

Chocolate is harvested and processed from a cocoa bean, where the cocoa butter fat is extracted.

Cocoa butter has a mixture of two types of fats, **A** and **B**.
A has a low melting point – **A**-type crystals of fat are soft and feel greasy.
B has a high melting point – **B**-type crystals impart gloss and 'snap.'

It is important to make sure that **A** and **B** crystals are completely melted to ensure a good gloss and avoid grey and white bloom. See below.

To get the chocolate ready for use, it needs to be tempered as follows:

- Heat the chocolate to 45°C.
- Remove from the heat.
- Cool the chocolate to 27°C.
- Then heat back up to 31-32°C for dark chocolate, 29-30°C for milk chocolate, and 27-28°C for white chocolate.

On setting, the whole mass will crystallize, which is known as 'seeding.'

There are two main faults in chocolate; these are referred to as bloom.

Grey bloom: A grey bloom forms on the surface. This is caused by dampness and condensation dissolving the surface sugar, which then recrystallizes on drying.

White bloom: A yellowish-white fat bloom, which is caused by bad tempering. So, take great care in tempering to ensure a good shine and good snap in the chocolate when broken.

Jams and curds

The difference between a jam and a curd is that the curd has the addition of butter and eggs. This gives a creamier texture. Lemon curd is delicious and the most common curd, but curds can be made from limes, oranges, and other fruits such as apples, rhubarb, or raspberries. Curds are not boiled but heated over a bain-marie (water bath) until the curd coats the back of a spoon. Jam is made from fruit and sugar and is boiled until the setting point is reached, where the jam begins to thicken, and the bubbles begin to plop sluggishly. It is the pectin in the fruit that helps to set the jam – if the pectin is low, then pectin can be added to aid setting. Pectin can be bought in most supermarkets.

Spices

Spices come from the seeds, bark, and roots of various plants. They can be dried and crushed to form a powder, or in some cases, like cinnamon and star anise, they can be kept whole. They are used as a flavouring, add colour, and in some cases, texture.

Herbs

These tend to be used as a garnish and are available in leaves, flowers, and stem. They are sometimes used as ingredients for bread or cake, e.g., lavender and rosemary. Fresh herbs tend to be less intense in flavour than dried.

Bread

Making good bread

This section explains some of the principles, processes, and ingredients of bread-making. It is worth reading through before you embark on a recipe!

Good bread can be made with just five ingredients: flour, yeast, salt, fat, and water. It is just magical taking these raw materials and creating something delicious. It has never left me; the wonder of watching a dough grow and the amazing smell of freshly baked bread. When I was training, I remember my father collecting me from college with my freshly baked bread and its aroma filling the car. We couldn't wait to get home, get some butter and lovely jam and sit and eat a banquet of fresh bread. Is there anything better?

Ingredients

Each ingredient has a specific role to play in the development of bread.

Flour: The flour needs to be strong because of the high level of proteins of glutenin and gliadin present. When the flour is hydrated and kneaded, the proteins are developed to form gluten. Then with continued kneading, it will produce a dough with an elastic, smooth consistency. When the yeast starts to do its job, creating carbon dioxide gas and ethyl alcohol, the dough is able to stretch and expand creating volume. Various flours can be used and contribute to flavour and texture: strong white, wholemeal, malted grains, granary, multi-seed, and country grain flour.

Yeast: Given the right conditions of food, moisture, time, and temperature, yeast will produce carbon dioxide gas and ethyl alcohol to create a light sponge-like texture. The yeast matures and develops by the fermentation of simple sugars naturally produced from the endosperm in the flour. This is broken down by simple sugars by the amylase enzyme, which is also naturally present in the flour. Temperature control also plays an important role in the fermentation process, which I will discuss later.

Salt: Salt contributes to flavour, helps control fermentation, and enhances colour. It is important to weigh salt and yeast separately as salt in direct contact with yeast will eliminate the yeast. Salt also helps to develop the gluten structure.

Fat: Adding a little fat to the dough helps hold the bubble structure stable and softens the crumb structure, gives nutritional value, and increases shelf life. In enriched doughs, such as bun goods and Danish, where the percentage of fat is higher, the yeast level may need to be increased.

Water: Water is an essential part of dough making and must be used in the right quantity to properly develop the gluten network in bread. If the dough has little or too much water, the gluten will not develop correctly, resulting in a lack of volume. The stronger the flour, the more water will be required in the dough.

The temperature of the water has an important part to play. A cold dough will be denser than a warm dough. The gassing activity of the yeast is dependent on time and temperature.

Dough temperature

Achieving the correct dough temperature is important to get the best fermentation. Too cold, and the dough will be too dense and too hot, and you risk damaging the yeast.

There is a simple calculation that will help you achieve the required temperature of your dough to around 26°C to 29°C (78°Fto 84°F), based on the temperature of the two main ingredients, flour and water.

Dough temperature calculation

Decide on your dough temperature. In this book, I have worked on a dough temperature of 26°C (78°F). Here is a worked example:

To calculate the necessary water temperature, double the required dough temperature, then subtract the flour temperature (i.e., room temperature). This will give you the temperature of water needed. When added to the rest of the ingredients, this will give you a dough temperature around 26°C (78°F).

Double the required dough temperature: 26°C x 2 = 52°C

The subtract the flour temperature of 20°C: 52°C - 20°C = 32°C. This will be the required water temperature.

Adding different ingredients

Depending on what you are making, you can add other ingredients to the dough to enrich it and contribute to the flavour, such as eggs, butter, spices, fruits, herbs, and pastes like tomato, pesto, cream cheese, as you will see in some of my recipes.

Bread making process

I have chosen to give you both the straight dough method, where all the ingredients are added at the start, and a pre-fermented dough method, which sometimes is referred to as starter dough.

Pre-ferment (starter) dough

Pre-ferment dough is where you start the dough with a percentage of flour, water, and a little yeast (no salt); mix together and leave the dough covered for anything from eight to sixteen hours at ambient temperature. This is then added to the main dough. A pre-ferment contributes to flavour and improves hydration and shelf life. It is well worth the planning.

Straight dough

Straight dough involves adding all dry ingredients together, then mixing in the water. Mix using a dough hook attachment. This hydrates the flour and develops the dough to a smooth elastic consistency.

Mixing

Mix the dough to develop the gluten kneading by hand to make a smooth elastic dough by lifting, turning, and applying some pressure. A tip here when mixing by hand: once moistened, knead into a ball, then relax the dough for a few minutes (have a cup of tea). Continue to knead. You will now notice as if by magic, the dough is softer and easier to handle to create a smooth elastic dough. If you are using a machine, a dough hook attachment is required; the dough will require approximately 10 minutes of mixing.

To check if the dough has been developed sufficiently, take a piece of dough and stretch it to create a thin see-through membrane that doesn't break. Think about when you put a piece of bubble gum in your mouth. If you try to blow a bubble straight away, it won't work. Put some energy in by chewing the bubble gum – the nature of the bubble gum changes to become pliable and stretchy – now you can blow a bubble. In the same way, you are preparing the dough so the yeast will do its job producing carbon dioxide gas and ethyl alcohol to expand the dough and create bubbles. The fat aligns itself around the bubbles, helping to stabilize the bubble structure.

Proving and baking

Bulk fermentation

This is where the dough is left to rise for the first time. Cover the dough and place it in a warm place to allow the dough to ferment. Most of my recipes in the book are based on a one-hour fermentation.

Knock back

This is where you knead the dough to knock out the gases which have developed. This equalizes the dough temperature and helps deliver the flavour. It also puts some strength back into the dough, which helps to improve the final loaf volume and texture. Leave the dough for a further 20 minutes before dividing and moulding.

Divide the dough

The dough can now be weighed into the units required for the product being made – hand mould the dough into balls and recover (this means to rest the dough) before its final shaping.

Final proof

After shaping, allow the dough to double in size. You can make a proving cabinet by placing a plastic box over the dough to keep it from 'skinning' (this is when the surface of the dough becomes dry and forms a skin.). Try to ensure it is in a warm place and cover it with an oiled plastic sheet. You will know when the dough is ready as it will slowly spring back when gently touched.

Dough cutting

If the dough is going to be cut, use either a small sharp knife or a blade. Hold the knife at a 45° angle and cut just below the skin in a clean sweep. Don't go too slowly, or the knife will drag and give you a rough edge. Cutting the dough helps to release the tension in the dough and helps it expand while baking, creating a pattern on the dough. Sometimes this is referred to as scoring.

Baking

Always pre-heat the oven.

Place a tray of water in the base of the oven to create steam, as this will help get volume and crusty bread. Sometimes I also spray water in the oven before closing the door.

An average loaf of 470g will take 25 minutes to bake; a larger loaf, say 920g, will take 40 minutes. The oven temperature can be 230°C (450°F)down to 200°C (400°F), depending on the sugar levels. The sweeter the goods, the cooler the oven is a good benchmark.

To check the bread is baked, tap the bottom, and the bread should sound hollow.

Cooling

If the bread is in a tin, remove it as soon as possible. Leaving the bread to cool in the tin will cause sweating, and the sides and base of the bread will be soggy. Sogginess will also encourage mould growth.

Freezing

Before freezing the bread, it should be completely cool and well-wrapped in a plastic bag.

The frozen bread should not be kept for longer than about 6 weeks in the freezer because it loses its flavour.

The crustiness of frozen bread can be revived by sprinkling the surface with water and placing it in a hot oven at 200°C (400°F) for about 10 minutes (small loaf).

Bread Fault Chart

This chart helps you identify faults in your bread. Faults are in the left-hand column and possible causes along the top.

Fault \ Cause	Lacks liquid	Too much liquid	Wrong flour	Too much flour	Not enough flour	Not enough yeast	Too much yeast	Under mixed dough	Overmixed dough	Skinning	Under baking	Over baking	Over proof	Under proof / cold proof	Poor moulding	Dough too soft	Dough too tight	Too much humidity	Not enough humidity	Not enough steam	Poor crust colour	Oven too cool	Oven too hot
Dough too tight	●		●	●																			
Dough too soft		●			●			●															
Poor volume						●								●	●								
Poor crust colour										●			●					●				●	
Excessive crust colour												●											●
Wrinkled surface			●				●							●								●	
Cobs not holding shape		●	●		●					●			●		●	●		●					
Mushroom top in tinned bread							●		●	●							●						
Cracks on the dough surface				●			●				●			●	●	●		●			●	●	
Skinning on the dough piece									●					●					●				
Streaks on surface / internal															●								
Holes under the top of the loaf								●	●	●			●		●	●		●					
Holes in internal crumb							●	●		●						●							
Crust too thick																			●				●

Cake

General principles

I am often asked what went wrong with my cake:

Why did it sink in the middle?
Why has the cake peaked and become dry?

The Fault Chart is useful to help you find solutions, but here is a little bit of information about the formula and balance of a cake that will also give you an insight.

The purpose of mixing is to disperse all ingredients as effectively as possible – using the correct mixing process to incorporate air into the mix, which will create texture and volume.

Weighing the ingredients correctly is key to producing a good cake.

I am reminded of a student who once weighed so much baking powder that the cake was climbing out of the tray onto the table and flowed out onto the floor!

Let us look at the role of each group of ingredients in a cake:

Group A: Flour and eggs help provide strength and structure to the cake.

Group B: Sugar, fat, and milk must be carried (i.e., supported) by the flour and the egg.

Group C: Sugars, fats, and baking powder help to open the structure of the cake and make it tender to eat.

Group D: Milk and water reduce lightness and can close the structure of the cake.

A balanced formula should contain enough materials from **Group B** as can be carried by **Group A**. These should be balanced against **Group C** and **Group D**.

Using this principle, there is enough strength provided by the eggs and flour to carry the sugar and the fat.

The closing effect of the fat and water in the eggs is balanced by the lifting effect of the fat and the air holding capacity of the eggs. Also, sugar has an opening effect on the structure. Up to 3% of baking powder may be used to open the crumb structure further.

The egg provides strength and structure BUT, in excess, produces a rubbery cake. The fat helps to aerate and shorten the structure of the cake. The egg and fat then produce opposite effects.

The role of the egg in cake recipe balance is more complex because it acts as both an aerating ingredient and as a liquid. Although more air may be beaten into the batter, it will not be held there. Instead, the batter will usually curdle because of the extra liquid. The cake produced will be heavier with a coarse crumb texture. The yolks give it a more pronounced colour.

Too much fat causes the batter to flow, producing a cake with a flat top. The texture is soft and greasy, and the crust will be soft and moist. There may be a slight heaviness at the base of the cake. The batter doesn't flow sufficiently, the cake has a raised peak, lacks volume, and the texture is dry and tough.

The table below summarises the effects of each ingredient on your cake.

Ingredient	Effects				
	Closing: produces heaviness	Lifting: produces aeration	Strength and structure	Greasiness	Shortens soft crumb
Fat	■	■		■	■
Water	■				
Eggs	■	■	■		
Flour	■		■		
Baking powder		■			

M fault and x fault

The two main recognised cake faults are referred to as the 'M' fault and the 'X' fault.

In the 'M' fault, if too much baking powder is used, the cake will sink in the centre. This fault occurs when any aerating or 'opening' ingredient is used in excess, causing the cake to rise more than the structure can support. The cell structure then breaks, releasing gas, and the centre collapses. The opening and closing agents act as opposites. For example, the 'M' fault can also be caused by using insufficient liquid. The same fault can be caused by using too much sugar. Excess sugar in a recipe produces a cake with a crisp top crust and a tendency to be dry. An 'M' fault may be corrected by using less sugar, less baking powder, or more liquid to balance the recipe.

In the 'X' fault, if too much of a closing agent, e.g., liquid, is used, the cake produced has a 'close' texture. That is, it is dense, tough, and rubbery. After baking, the sides tend to collapse inwards, forming a sort of 'X' shape called an 'X' fault. There is often a region of very dense crumb texture or 'bone' near the bottom of the cake. Cakes demonstrating an 'X' fault usually have too much liquid in the batter. As the extra water turns to steam, it aerates the structure beyond endurance, causing it to collapse.

While it is in the oven, the cake volume is usually good, but as the cake cools after baking, the steam condenses and stops supporting the crumb structure. The cake then begins to shrink and collapse, especially at the sides. As there is more liquid present, the starch gelatinises quickly and fully, giving a rubbery crumb texture. A cake with an 'X' fault can be improved by reducing the liquid or increasing the sugar or baking powder.

Cake making methods

Creaming method

This can also be referred to as the Sugar Batter Process.

This method is used for a wide variety of cakes, lemon, chocolate, coffee, Genoese bases, and fruit cakes.

Key point: All ingredients should be at room temperature (approximately 21°C or 70°F). Butter straight from the fridge is difficult to cream because the structure is too hard – it creams better at room temperature. Eggs that are too cold when being added to a batter that is at room temperature will cause the mixture to curdle (sometimes known as 'splitting'). Place the cracked eggs in a jug and put them in warm water to take off the chill.

Creaming process

Cream the butter and sugar well, until light in colour as well as texture. This is to aerate the cake batter. The sugar dissolves in the butter whilst it is creaming.

Scrape down the bowl as necessary to ensure complete blending of the ingredients.

Add the beaten egg gradually to the creamed fat and sugar, beating well between each addition to avoid the mixture curdling (splitting). This can be done over four egg additions. If there are signs of curdling, add a couple of table spoons of flour from the weighed ingredients – this will help rebind the batter.

Sieve all the dry ingredients together to break up any lumps. Add the dry ingredients and mix carefully to avoid toughening and to maintain aeration. The aim is to get a smooth batter, and its consistency should be dropping, i.e., when the mixture gently drops from the spoon. This can be adjusted at the end with a little milk. If there is fruit in the recipe, add the fruit by hand to avoid damaging the cake batter or the fruit.

Foam-based cakes

Foam-based cakes are light and can be fat-free. They rely on whipped eggs and sugar to create a foam. The flour is folded in by hand once the foam has been created, being careful not to over-mix and collapse the sponge. Melted butter can be folded in at the end if required. Different textures can be achieved by whisking the whites separated from the yolks.

Tin and tray preparation

It is important to prepare your tins and trays for the cake before you start to mix. Preparation will depend on the type of cake you are making. The aim is to ensure that the cake can be removed from the tin or tray without being damaged. For high-fat cakes, the tin can be sprayed with fat, and a parchment disc placed in the base of the tin. Rich fruit cakes will need parchment lining on the sides of the tin as well as the base. They may also need a protective paper layer attached around the outside of the tin. This helps to prevent the fruit from burning on the sides of the cake due to the sugar content of the fruit. Some Bundt tin-type moulds can be greased and floured. Foam-based cakes, e.g., Swiss rolls, need to have a parchment lining on the base of the tin. For foam-based cakes, the sides of the tin can be greased and floured, again with a parchment disc at the base.

Baking

Always pre-heat the oven before placing the cake inside. Thinner cakes may need a slightly higher temperature but baked for less time, for example, Swiss rolls (200°C or 190°C fan; 400°F, Gas 6). The sweeter the goods, the lower the oven – rich fruit cakes are baked at lower temperatures but baked for longer (150°C or 130°C fan; 300°F, Gas 2). Most loaf-type cakes (180°C or 170°C fan; 350°F, Gas 4) take 25 to 40 minutes to bake. Don't open the oven too soon otherwise, the cake will collapse as it hasn't set.

Test for baking

The last part of the cake to be baked is the top centre. Test for baking at the centre of the cake by pressing gently with your finger – the cake should spring back when it is ready. A fine needle cake tester can be used and should come out clean when inserted in the middle of the cake.

Cake Fault Chart

This chart helps you identify faults in your cake. Faults are in the left-hand column and possible causes along the top.

Fault	Under baking time	Over baking time	Oven temp too low	Oven temp too high	Excessive sugar	Excessive fat	Too much moisture agent	Too much Baking Powder	Too much flour	Insufficient baking powder	Insufficient moisture agent	Disturbing before baking	Weak flour	Strong flour	Toughened batter	Under beating	Over beating	Insufficient sugar	Fruit too moist	Insufficient steam in oven
Sinking in the centre	X			X	X		X	X				X					X			
Wet steam under crust	X											X								
Wet seam at base			X				X												X	
Peaked tops				X							X			X	X					X
Cauliflower tops				X																X
Poor volume	X			X	X		X	X	X	X				X		X		X		X
Shrinkage / loose bands																				
Spots on crust					X			X			X									X
Close bound crumb									X	X	X			X		X	X			
Loose woolly texture				X				X		X						X				
Course dry texture		X	X						X		X						X			
Uneven texture		X	X				X	X	X		X		X		X	X	X	X		X
Poor keeping qualities			X				X											X		
Poor oven colour			X		X													X		
Excessive oven colour				X	X															X
Thick crust	X	X		X							X						X	X	X	
Sunken fruit	X	X	X	X			X					X	X	X	X		X		X	X

Cake Faults Pictures

The cake can be assessed in two ways:

The **External Appearance:** This is where we refer to the crust, colour, and volume.

The **Internal Appearance:** This is where we look at the crumb structure, colour, texture, and, of course, aroma.

I have made some fault cakes to help you identify problems. There are more, but this will give you some guidelines.

Control cake

- Good split on top.
- Even colour.
- Good volume.
- Thin crust around the edge.
- Even crumb structure.
- Good aroma.
- Cuts well and is moist.

Cake with strong flour

- Colour is a bit pale.
- Has an uneven split on the top.
- Sides cave in slightly.
- Thick crust, with a core at the top of the cake.
- Crumb structure has holes.
- When cut, the cake is tough and dry.
- Strong flour aroma.

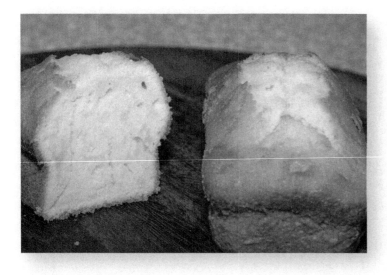

Cake with high-fat levels

- Lacks colour.
- Uneven split – ragged.
- Lacks volume.
- Crust thin when cut.
- Close crumb structure with elongated holes.
- Greasy to touch.
- Leaves a greasy feel in the mouth.
- Poor aroma.

Cake with excess liquid

- Colour is not too bad.
- Lacks volume.
- Very close crumb structure.
- Core under the top.
- Moist cake and sticky when cut.
- Sometimes there will be a core at the base of the cake.

Cake with too much baking powder

- Darker crust colour.
- Even split on top.
- Thick crust and dark on the sides when cut.
- Sides beginning to collapse.
- Open crumb structure, some tunnelling holes.
- Cake is dry and has an acidic taste.

Shortcrust and Sweet Pastry

Pastry methods

There are two main methods to follow when making pastry – Rubbing in or Creaming. The choice will depend on how rich you want the pastry to be.

Rubbing in method (for shortcrust pastry)

In this method, the fat is rubbed into the flour to resemble breadcrumbs before adding the liquid to bind the pastry. The reason for rubbing the fat into the flour is to prevent the protein gluten strands from developing. This helps to limit the amount of water the flour absorbs and helps to shorten the paste. However, if soft butter is used rather than cold butter, then the flour and fat can form a paste quickly, and adding liquid can be difficult, which will lead to toughness in the pastry.

When making shortcrust pastry, two approaches can be used. Either:

- butter and shortening (vegetable fat) or
- butter and lard (animal fat).

This helps to shorten the pastry and helps with crispness.

Do not be fooled!

I remember when a student with hot hands rubbed the fat into the flour to the point that the pastry bound together to a paste but without the water. Then, thinking the pastry was ok, proceeded to roll it out: impossible – the paste just crumbled and fell apart!

The water is needed to bind the paste together to make it pliable.

Creaming method (for sweet pastry)

This method is followed where there is a higher fat, sugar, and egg content in the recipe. Cream the fat and sugar until light and creamy; then the egg is added gradually, creating a batter to fold in the flour and mix to form a paste.

Key points

- Always weigh ingredients carefully.
- Always use cold butter.
- Rest the pastry when made for at least 30 minutes before processing.
- Rest before baking to eliminate the possible shrinking of the pastry.
- Don't overwork the pastry, as it will toughen and become difficult to handle, and ultimately the texture will be tough when eating.

Additions

You can make changes to the pastry, by exchanging some of the flour for other ingredients such as ground almonds, ground hazel nuts, ground coconut, or cocoa powder.

Sugar can be changed from caster sugar to icing sugar. This will give a melt-in-the-mouth feel.

For savoury shortcrust, salt, pepper, mustard, or parmesan cheese can be added for flavour.

Baking blind

This refers to preparing a pastry case for a filling.

- Grease the flan ring.
- Line it with the rolled-out pastry ensuring the sides are attached to the ring.
- Cut the pastry to get nice sharp, clean edges.
- Line the flan with a greaseproof paper disc and fill it with baking beans. (I use lentils – you could also use rice. Keep them in a jar for baking, and they can be used repeatedly.)
- Chill the flan before baking, then bake for 15 minutes; this sets the flan sides.
- Then remove the beans and greaseproof paper, return the flan to the oven and complete the baking.

The case is now ready for the next process.

Shortcrust and Sweet Pastry Fault Chart

This chart helps you identify faults in your shortcrust and sweet pastry. Faults are in the left-hand column and possible causes along the top.

Fault	Insufficient fat/egg/sugar	Flour too strong	Poor rolling technique	Not enough moistening agent	Too much moistening agent	Not enough rest before baking	Not enough aeration	Too much aeration	Oven temperature too high	Oven temperature too low	Not enough fat/egg used	Too much fat used	Too much sugar or wrong sugar used	Not enough sugar used	Undermixing	Over mixing	Undissolved sugar
Tough pastry	■	■	■	■	■					■		■				■	
Shrinkage		■	■		■	■											
Distorted shape	■	■	■	■	■	■									■	■	
Poor texture	■	■					■	■							■	■	■
Too much colour									■				■				
Not enough colour	■									■				■	■		
Pastry too short								■			■						
Brown spots on crust									■				■				■

Puff Pastry

Puff pastry is made by a process of aeration by lamination – that is, the fat is incorporated through the dough by rolling, turning, and creating layers.

The dough rises because of the steam that is created by the water in the fat which is used between the layers. Strong flour is used to make the dough. Also, a little fat is used in the base dough to help modify the gluten structure so that it is more extensible and relaxed. It is more able to cope with the lamination process and encourages a good lift.

English method

Roll out the dough into a rectangle of 30 x 15cm (12 x 6").

Soften the fat and spread it over two-thirds of the dough (the hatched area in the diagram below).

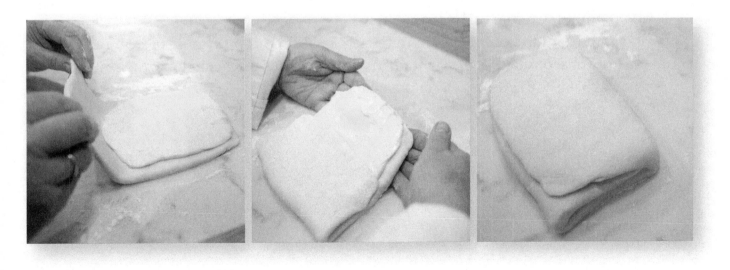

<u>First picture</u>: Fold one-third of the dough, which has no fat on it to cover half the fat.

<u>Second picture</u>: Fold the other third over the top.

<u>Third picture</u>: This shows the fat enclosed in the dough. This is effectively a ½ turn.

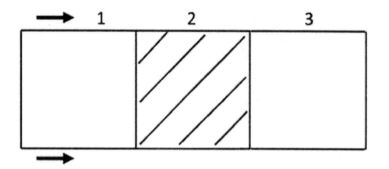 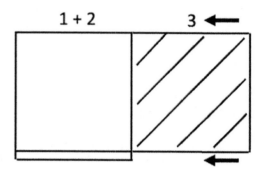

Once the '**dough**' above has been folded to enclose its fat, it is called the '**paste**,' and that's the term we use from here on in this method.

Turning the paste

The paste will need 6½ turns. Keep the seam of the paste always on the left.

- Roll the paste to the same rectangle size (30 x 15cm (12 x 6")) and fold in three.
- Wrap the paste in a plastic bag so that it doesn't skin over. Rest the paste in the fridge for 15 minutes before each turn.
- It is important to keep the seam to the left each time you turn the paste to ensure the paste has been rolled in the right direction. If this has not been done, the result will be an oval bake as opposed to a round bake.

French method

<u>First picture</u>: Form a dough ball, shape it into a square, then roll out each of the points to form a cross, as in the diagram below. The dough will be slightly raised in the centre.

<u>Second picture</u>: Soften the fat and shape it into a square. Place the fat in the square centre of the cross on the raised dough.

<u>Third picture</u>: Fold each corner over the fat, ensuring the fat is completely enclosed. Once the fat is enclosed, as with the English Method, and the '**dough**' above has been folded to enclose its fat, it is called the '**paste**,' and that's the term we use from here on in this method.

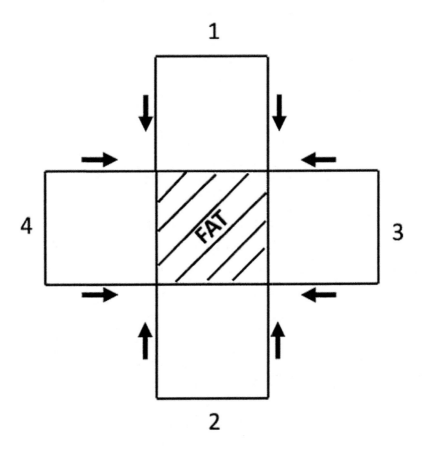

Now continue to roll out the paste into the rectangle, as described in **"Turning the paste"** above in order to create layers.

Alternatively, you can do four book turns. The term **"Book turn"** means rolling the paste into a rectangle. Mark the centre line, then bring each of the two ends to meet at the centre line and then fold together as in the picture below.

Scotch method

This is sometimes referred to as the Blitz method. It is a quick method and is suitable for sausage rolls, pasties, and pie tops.

Cut the fat into small cubes of about 1 cm; add flour, salt, and cold iced water. Mix together, making sure the large fat cubes are visible. Flour your table and roll the pastry. Fold and turn as described in **"Turning the paste"** to create the layers.

Turns for all methods

You can choose to do either 6 half turns or 4 book turns.

Understanding the quality of your pastry

When all the layers have been completed, and the paste is cut, you can see the layers of fat and dough. In the picture above, I have cut across the folds and propped it up on the parent product. This allows you to see the line between the folds where the fat has been incorporated. You will see that the line is thin – this is because I have used butter as my fat, and it has been spread thinly through the dough. The appearance in the picture is what you should be aiming for.

Baking

Correct baking is essential and should be done in a pre-heated hot oven.

The oven temperature will depend on the product. For products containing fillings or are sugar topped, bake between 210-220°C and 205-215°C fan (420-450°F), Gas 7.

For plain and unfilled products, bake between 210-230°C and 205-220°C fan (425-450°F), Gas 7-8.

Faults occur if the oven is too cool. The fat leaks out, and the product does not lift and will not be crisp. It is important to allow at least 20 minutes of baking with the door shut to ensure the lift in the pastry and to allow the pastry to set. Opening the door too soon will cause the pastry to collapse and become doughy in texture.

Puff Pastry Fault Chart

This chart helps you identify faults in your puff pastry. Faults are in the left-hand column and possible causes along the top.

Cause \ Fault	Uneven lift	Poor volume	Distorted shape	Shrinkage	Loss of fat during baking	Tough eating	Cores	Filling spilling out	Skinning
Incorrect rolling technique	X		X				X		
Fat unevenly distributed	X			X					
Not enough rest before baking	X		X					X	
Uneven heat distribution in the oven	X		X		X				
Too many turns given									
Pastry rolled too thinly				X					
Fat too soft to process					X				
Process temperature too high		X			X		X		
Too much fat					X				
Not enough fat									
Oven temperature too low		X			X			X	
Incorrect cutting and shaping	X	X	X					X	
Flour too soft		X							
Flour too strong				X					
Dough too tight									
Dough too soft		X		X					
Skinning		X					X		
Not enough turns given		X			X				
Paste left uncovered									X
Poor glazing/sealing	X		X					X	X
Overfilling the product								X	

Meringues

Many people are anxious about making meringues, so let me take away the fear. There are some key points that you need to follow.

Meringue is a mixture of whisked egg whites (albumen, which is the protein) and sugar.

Caster sugar is used, as the grains are finer and are more easily suspended in the bubbles of the whisked egg whites.

Key points

Sterilise the bowls and whisks – they **MUST** be grease free.

> *I remember marking a student's work on key points of making meringue and they stated that it was most important to sterilise your* **bowels** *before starting!*

The easiest way to make meringues is by machine with the whisk attachment, or a hand machine, as more air can be incorporated.

There must be no traces of yolk in the whites, as the yolk contains fat and will cause the meringue to lack volume and drop.

Sugar is heavy, so add the sugar slowly so it dissolves in the egg white and will stabilise the meringue. If it is added too quickly, the whites will struggle to get volume, and they will be soft and won't hold shape when the meringue is piped.

The aim is to increase the volume and have stability in the meringue.

Egg whites straight from the fridge do not whip well. They are best at room temperature – about 21°C (68°F).

An over-whisked meringue will make the foam dry – it will break down and weep.

The meringue needs to be piped or used immediately.

Meringue methods

There are three methods for making meringue: Swiss, French, and Italian.

Swiss method – Hot

This will be denser and more stable than French meringue. It makes a great base for butter-cream.

- One-part egg whites to two parts sugar.
- Put the sugar and eggs into a clean bowl.
- Combine the ingredients with a hand whisk
- Place the bowl over a saucepan of hot water (40-50°C or 110-120°F) and whisk to dissolve the sugar; test for grains – it should be smooth.
- Remove from the heat. Transfer to a machine with a whisk.
- Whisk on top speed until a stiff peak is achieved.
- The meringue is now ready for processing and baking.

French method – Cold

This is the most common method and ideal for pie topping and mousses.

- One-part egg whites to two parts sugar.
- Whisk the egg whites in a clean bowl with 10% of the sugar on top speed until the volume is tripled.
- Add the sugar in a slow stream whilst the machine is still on a medium speed.
- Mix until all the sugar has been incorporated.
- Use as required.

Italian method – Boiled

This method is very versatile and is great for all products.

- Put 300gm of sugar and 90ml of water in a clean saucepan.
- Follow the sugar boiling principles (see below) and boil to 118°C or 245°F.
- Whisk the egg whites to form a foam.

- Add the boiled sugar carefully on slow speed.
- Whisk on medium speed until the meringue is cold and forms stiff peaks.
- Use as required.

Adding colour and flavour to meringue

Adding colour and flavour to meringue is possible. Use liquid colour; add it at the end before piping. Colour can also be added into the piping bag to create streaks in the meringue when piped.

Meringue can be dusted with cocoa powder, desiccated coconut, or nibbed nuts for texture.

Preparing trays for baking

Line the baking tray with parchment paper. Designs can be drawn on the paper, and then you can turn the paper upside down before piping for accurate sizes.

Baking the meringue

Always pre-heat the oven to 120°C, 110°C fan (around 240°F) and Gas 1.

Depending on the size, baking can be 30 minutes or longer. The meringue piece should be lifted easily off the parchment when baked. If the oven is too hot, the meringue will expand and may weep. It will also, of course, colour quickly and caramelize.

Sugar boiling principles

The ingredients required for sugar boiling are 660g granulated or cube sugar, 240g glucose syrup and 240g water, and a pinch of cream of tartar. The glucose is made from starch such as maize and helps to slow down the crystallization of the sugar.

Place the sugar with the water in a saucepan, melt the sugar, and heat gently to boiling point. At this stage, add the glucose and boil rapidly.

Do not allow the sugar crystals to form around the side of the pan, as they will fall into the pot and crystallise the whole mass. To avoid this, brush water around the side of the saucepan, and any forming crystals will dissolve.

The water is driven off, and the sugar thickens and begins to colour. The sugar can be used at different stages, depending on what you are using it for.

A sugar thermometer is highly recommended to achieve the correct temperature.

I am reminded as I write this of being taught to check the temperatures below with a bowl of iced water. I had to dip my fingers in the iced water, then into the boiling sugar, and then directly into the iced water to check whether the sugar was a thread or soft ball. How scary was that? Thankfully health and safety do not recommend this practice.

Invest in a thermometer!

Sugar boiling temperatures

- 108-112°C (226-232°F) – Thread
- 112-115°C (232-235°F) – Strong thread
- 118°C (244°F) – Soft ball Italian meringue
- 125°C (257°F) – Hard ball Italian meringue
- 140°C (284°F) – Soft crack rock sugar
- 148°C (292°F) – Spun sugar, nougat, glazed fruits, poured sugar, pulled sugar
- 150°C (300°F) – Crack
- 165°C (330°F) – Caramel, dark nougat

Meringue Fault Chart

This chart helps you identify faults in your meringue. Faults are in the left-hand column and possible causes along the top.

Fault	Equipment is not sterile	Trace of grease	Under whipped	Over whipped	Mixer set too high	Cold whites	Add an acid cream of tartar or lemon juice	Undissolved sugar	Sugar too course	Whisk too heavy/thick spindles	Oven too hot	Oven too cool	Over baked	Under baked	Poor piping skills
Meringue too soft	■		■	■		■	■			■		■			
Lacks volume	■	■								■				■	
Heavy and shiny		■	■			■	■		■	■					
Collapsed when sugar was added					■			■	■	■					
Base dark when baked											■		■		
Weeping meringues			■	■				■					■	■	
Meringues blown				■							■				
Meringues distorted			■							■		■			■

Why Is Weighing So Important?

A uniform product needs to be produced each day. Even small differences in weighed ingredients can lead to failure.

For example, chefs can make soup, but if they are short of an onion or celery, they can make adjustments by adding herbs, and in the end, they will still have a soup.

On the other hand, bakers are chemists in the bakery, and for successful and consistent results, they follow formulae that require accurate measurements – there is no room for guesswork. Therefore, understanding the functions of ingredients is important.

Density is a measure of the compactness of particles or molecules in a liquid or solid.

Viscosity is a measure of how easily a liquid will flow. If liquid particles or molecules slide past each other easily, the flow is quicker – if they bump into each other, the flow is slower.

Volume is a measure of dry or liquid using scales, cups, spoons, or jugs.

Below are weight, volume, and spoon measures (Spoon measures are good when the scales don't read low numbers. I have used these in recipes to help with accuracy).

Always check that the scales are clean and in good working order before weighing each ingredient, e.g., batteries are not running low. If you are weighing multiple ingredients into the same bowl, ensure that the scales go back to zero each time.

Weights Metric and Imperial

Metric	Imperial	Metric	Imperial
15g	½ oz	150g	5½ oz
20g	¾ oz	175g	6oz
30g	1oz	200g	7oz
40g	1½ oz	225g	8oz
50g	1¾ oz	250g	9oz
60g	2oz	300g	10oz
75g	2½ oz	450g	1lb
85g	3oz	500g	1lb 2oz
100g	3½ oz	675g	1½lb
115g	4oz	900g	2lb
125g	4½ oz	1kg	2¼lb
140g	5oz	1.5kg	3lb 3oz

Volume Measurements

Metric	Imperial	Metric	Imperial
30ml	1fl oz	450ml	15fl oz
60ml	2fl oz	500ml	16 fl oz
75ml	2½fl oz	600ml	1 pint
100ml	3½fl oz	750ml	1¼ pints
120ml	4fl oz	900ml	1½ pints
150ml	5fl oz (¼ pint)	1litre	1¾ pints
175ml	6fl oz	1.2litres	2 pints
200ml	7fl oz	1.4litres	2½ pints
240ml	8fl oz	1.5litres	2¾ pints
300ml	10fl oz (½ pint)	1.7litres	3 pints
350ml	12fl oz	2litres	3½ pints
400ml	14fl oz	3litres	5¼ pints

Spoon Measurements

Teaspoon (tsp) and tablespoon (tbsp) measurements are useful when small amounts are required.

Spoon size	Metric	Ml
1 tbsp	15g	15ml
½ tbsp	7.5g	7.5ml
1 tsp	5g	5ml
¾ tsp	3.7g	3.7ml
½ tsp	2.5g	2.5ml
¼ tsp	1.25g	1.25ml
⅛ tsp	0.62g	0.62ml

Length measurements

Metric	Imperial
3mm	⅛"
6mm	¼"
1cm	½"
2cm	¾"
6cm	2½"
8cm	3"
10cm	4"
13cm	5"
15cm	6"
18cm	7"
20cm	8"
23cm	9"
25cm	10"
30cm	12"

Oven Temperatures

It is always advisable to pre-heat the oven before baking. If you are unsure of the temperature gauges on the oven, I recommend getting a thermometer that can be placed in the oven to get a reading.

Celsius	Celsius fan	Fahrenheit	Gas	Description
110°C	100°C	225°F	¼	Cool
130°C	120°C	250°F	½	Cool
140°C	130°C	275°F	1	Very low
150°C	140°C	300°F	2	Very low
160°C	150°C	325°F	3	Low
180°C	170°C	350°F	4	Moderate
190°C	180°C	375°F	5	Moderately hot
200°C	190°C	400°F	6	Hot
220°C	210°C	425°F	7	Hot
230°C	220°C	450°F	8	Very hot
240°C	230°C	475°F	9	Very hot

Tin and Tray Preparation for Baking

Releasing agents are required to help separate the products from trays, tins, and pans. These are the methods:

Bread tins:

Grease with melted fat. Ensure the corners are coated – do not over-grease – we are not deep frying! This can be done by hand using a brush. Tins can be sprayed – aim properly, so you cover the area fully.

Sponge tins:

Grease and flour the sides, then place a parchment disc on the base. Some tins are silicone coated and do not need further treatment as they are non-stick.

Some tins may need to be lined with paper cases. Parchment is best. Greaseproof paper can be used, but it needs to be greased, so the product doesn't stick to the paper.

A silicone sheet is a non-stick baking mat that can be used to line trays. These can be washed in soapy water, dried after baking, and used repeatedly.

Cleanliness:

Always ensure that the trays and tins are clean so there are no signs of cross-contamination between products.

SPRING

The spring green shoots,
Blossom on the trees,
Snowdrops peeking through
Heralding new life and hope
A time for plans and projects.

A collection of seasonal recipes
to make, bake, and enjoy

Apricot, Chocolate, and Almond Tray Bake

This tray bake is delicious; the white chocolate works so well with the apricot.

Equipment: Scales, measuring spoons, saucepan, spatula, bowl, baking tray 30 x 20cm (12 x 8") lined with parchment, sharp knife, ruler.

Oven: Pre-heat to 180°C, 170°C fan, (375°F); Gas 5.

Apricot jam — Group A

200g	Dried apricots	
1 zest & juice	Lemon	
100ml	Water	
200g	Granulated sugar	

- Slice the dried apricots.
- Place in the saucepan with 100ml of water and the zest and juice of the lemon.
- Cook until the apricots are soft and most of the water has gone; about 10 minutes.
- Add the granulated sugar; dissolve, then boil until the setting point (The bubbles will slowly pop when it is nearly ready). It will take about 15 minutes.
- Allow to cool.

Pastry base — Group B

225g	Plain flour
5g (1 tsp)	Baking powder
100g	Caster sugar
85g	Soft brown sugar
225g	Unsalted butter

- Place the flour, caster sugar, soft brown sugar, and baking powder in a bowl; blend together.
- Cut the butter into cubes and rub the butter through the dry mix to form a crumble.
- Weigh 260g and place in a bowl for the topping.
- Place the rest of the crumble onto the baking tray and evenly press down to level.
- Bake 15 minutes.
- When baked, cool before the next stage.

Assembly — Group C

260g	of the above crumble
250g	Apricot jam
100g	White chocolate baking chips
40g	Flaked almonds

- Take the warm apricot jam from Group A and spread it over the cooled baked base from Group B.
- Sprinkle the top with 50g of white chocolate chips.
- Add 20g of the flaked almonds into the remaining crumble and sprinkle over the top of the apricot jam filling.
- Sprinkle the remainder of the flaked almonds and chocolate over the crumble.
- Place in the oven for the final bake for 20 minutes.
- Remove from the oven and allow to go cold in the tray.

Apricot Jane's

Hints and Tips

- The homemade jam has more textured than bought jam and gives more texture when eating.

- The filling could be changed to a jam of your choice.

- The Baker's chocolate chips are baked stable, i.e., the chocolate holds its shape during baking.

- The chocolate could also be milk or dark.

Oatmeal, Carrot, and Raisin Cookies

This recipe was developed using California raisins which are sun-dried and delicious. The oats, desiccated coconut, and carrots help to give an interesting texture to this cookie.

Equipment:	Scales, measuring spoons, mixing bowls, spatula, scraper, jug, grater, baking tray 30 x 20cm (12 x 8"), baking parchment.
Oven:	Pre-heat to 180°C, 170°C fan (350°F); Gas 4.
Yield:	20 cookies at 60g.

Group A

250g	Caster sugar	• Cream together the butter and sugar until light and creamy.
300g	Softened butter	

Group B

1	Egg	• Bend together the egg, golden syrup, vanilla, and cream.
30g	Golden syrup	• Add in two stages to Group A.
50g	Cream	• Scrape down the bowl between additions to ensure a fully mixed batter.
½ tsp	Vanilla	

Group C

90g	Rolled oats	• Fold the flour, coconut, and oats into the batter.
290g	Plain four	• Add the grated carrot and raisins; mix to ensure all ingredients are combined.
90g	Desiccated coconut	• Weigh the mix into 60g units; roll into balls, and place on a prepared tray. Flatten the tops a little. Allow space between them as the mix will flow a little.
150g	Grated carrots	• Bake for 20 minutes.
250g	Raisins	• Remove from the oven and allow to cool on the tray as they will be fragile until set.

Apricot Jane's
Hints and Tips

- Dip the table spoon in warm water, then dip into the golden syrup. It is easier to weigh as the golden syrup will slip off the spoon.

- You can change the caster sugar to golden caster, but soft brown sugars darken the crumb.

- The raisins could be soaked in 1tbsp rum, which would give extra flavour.

Hazelnut and Chocolate French Madeleines

The hazelnuts go so well with chocolate. I thought it would work well as a Madeleine, a lovely light sponge delight.

Equipment:	Scales, measuring spoons, madeleine shell moulds, bowl, spatula, sieve, whisk, saucepan, piping bag, plain piping tube 1.5cm, cooling wire, thermometer.
Oven:	Pre-heat to 180°C, 170°C fan (350°F); Gas 4.
Yield:	15 Madeleines.

Sponge A + B

Group A

65g	Butter	• Melt the butter and turn to beurre noisette – a brown butter, not burnt – the colour of nuts. When ready, the butter stops sizzling. • Leave to cool.

Group B

60g	Icing sugar	• Place the hazelnuts on parchment and roast in the oven for about 10 minutes. This adds to the flavour.
40g	Ground hazelnuts	• Sieve the flour, icing sugar, and cocoa powder into a bowl.
40g	Plain flour	• Add the cool roasted ground hazelnuts; blend together.
15g	Cocoa powder	• Add the egg whites, honey, and vanilla; whisk together with the beurre noisette.
90g (3)	Egg whites	• Mix together thoroughly to create a smooth batter.
2 tsp	Honey	• Cover with cling film and leave in the fridge for 40 minutes.
1 tsp	Vanilla	

Process

- Grease and lightly dust in flour on the madeleine shell moulds.
- Place the madeleine batter into a piping bag.
- Evenly pipe into the prepared madeleine tins.
- Bake for 15-20 minutes.
- When baked, place on a cooling wire.

Topping		Group C
200g	Dark chocolate couverture	• Melt the chocolate in a bowl over hot water to 45°C (113°F).
		• Remove from the heat and cool to 26°C (78°F).
		• Heat back up to 31°C (87°F).
		• The chocolate is ready for use.
		• Dip the fluted side of the shell in the chocolate; clear the edges with your finger so there are no drips.
		• Allow to set.

Apricot Jane's

Hints and Tips

• Placing the mixture into the fridge helps to firm up the butter and makes it easier to deposit into the tin.

• You can change the ground hazelnut to almond and use the zest of lemon if you prefer.

• If cocoa is not required, exchange it for plain flour.

• The madeleines can be just dusted in icing sugar.

• A lovely moist sponge delight!

Hot Cross Buns

On Good Friday morning in the bakery, we sprinkled liquid bun spice and warm water on the pavement outside around the entrance to the shop. The spicy aroma smell drew in the customers.

Equipment:	Scales, measuring spoons, bowl for dough, scraper, baking trays, jug for liquids, piping bag, scissors, paint brush, saucepan, whisk, cooking thermometer.
Oven:	Pre-heat to 200°C, 190°C fan (400°F); Gas 6.
Dough temperature:	26°C (78°F). See Hints and Tips.
Yield:	18 x 60g buns.

Dough   Group A

500g	Strong flour	• Sift together all the dry ingredients: flour, salt, sugar, milk powder.
4g (¾ tsp)	Salt	• Rub the butter into the dry ingredients.
80g	Sugar	
80g	Butter	

Group B

14g (2 sachets)	Dried yeast	• Mix the yeast into the warm milk to disperse.
50ml	Milk	• Add the water, yeast, milk, and eggs to the dry ingredients and work to form a dough.
200ml	Warm water	• Knead for about 10 minutes until the dough is developed. It will be smooth and elastic.
2 (medium)	Eggs	• Place the dough in a bowl and cover with cling film which has been oiled and prove for 1 hour in a warm place.

Group C

100g	Raisins	• Knock back the dough; add the fruit, and rest for 15 minutes to allow it to recover. To prevent the dough skinning, cover with the oiled cling film.
80g	Currants	• Weigh the dough into 60g portions and hand mould each into a ball. Allow it to recover again for 5 minutes and then re-mould and place in rows onto a tray that is greased or lined with silicone paper.
20g	Mixed peel	
10g (2 tsp)	Mixed spice	
1	Orange zest and juice	• Prove for about 20 to 30 minutes in a warm place; the buns will double in size.

Crossing paste		Group D
100g	Plain flour	• Rub the shortening into the dry ingredients, then add the water. Whisk until smooth.
20g	Shortening (e.g., Trex)	• Place the mixture into a piping bag; cut a small hole in the bag.
Pinch each of	Salt and baking powder	• When the buns are proved, carefully pipe a line across the buns. This will be easier if your buns are all placed in rows and then across the first row to form a cross over each bun.
40ml	Milk	• Bake for about 15 minutes and a nice golden colour is achieved with the white cross.
80ml	Water	• When removing from the oven, tap the tray to eliminate any air bubbles.

Glaze		Group E
160g	Sugar	• Place the water, sugar, lemon, and cinnamon stick in a saucepan.
60ml	Water	• Dissolve the sugar and bring to a boil; turn off the heat.
½	Lemon juice	• Brush over the buns with this glaze.
½	Cinnamon stick	

Apricot Jane's
Hints and Tips

• Dough temperature is important to achieve the best results. The yeast works best at 26°C. This is explained fully in the Section on Bread on page 15.

• This is an enriched dough with Butter, sugar, milk, and egg, so the yeast amount is higher than it would be for a plain dough.

• It is best to add the fruit at the knockback stage so that it doesn't get damaged. Adding the spice later encourages early fermentation as spices can slow down yeast activity.

- When kneading into balls, apply a small amount of pressure. Arch your hand, and as you move the dough around, you will feel it spring up. The dough should be smooth.

- Tapping the tray on removal from the oven helps to eliminate any trapped air bubbles and will stop the bun from wrinkling.

- Trex is a brand of what is called 'shortening.' Other brands are available.

- In Group C, we allow the dough to recover before the next stage. Otherwise, it stretches and tears. See also the Section on Bread, page 15.

Rhubarb and Custard Crumble Tart

When rhubarb is in season, try this tart. The sharpness and creaminess are a delight, and it has become a family favourite.

Equipment:	Scales, measuring spoons, bowl for pastry, frying pan, spatula, jug, 20cm (8") round perforated flan tin, rolling pin, whisk, baking beans.
Yield:	Pre-heat to 180°C, 170°C fan (350°F); Gas 4.

Pastry		Group A
140g	Plain flour	• Rub the butter into the flour with a zest of lemon.
65g	Butter	• Mix the sugar and egg together.
50g	Caster sugar	• Add the sugar and egg into the flour crumble and mix to form a smooth paste.
50g (1)	Egg	• Wrap in cling film and rest in the fridge for 15 minutes.
½	Zest of lemon	

Process

- Roll out the pastry to 3mm thick and line a pre-greased flan tin; trim the edges at the top for a clean finish.
- Line the flan with greaseproof paper cartouche and fill with baking beans.
- Chill in the fridge for 10 minutes before baking for 20 minutes.
- Remove the baking beans and return to the oven to dry out at the same temperature for about 5 minutes. The pastry will feel dry when touched.

Filling		Group B
50g	Caster sugar	• Trim the leaves and end piece off the rhubarb and wash thoroughly.
350g	Rhubarb	• Cut into 3cm (1") pieces.
½	Juice of lemon	• Place the sugar and lemon in the frying pan and the pieces of rhubarb on top of the sugar.
		• Heat gently to dissolve the sugar.
		• The rhubarb will create juices, gently turn the rhubarb, DO NOT ALLOW IT TO BREAK DOWN.
		• Turn off the heat and leave to cool.

Custard		Group C
1 large	Egg	• Mix the sugar, flour, egg, and yolk together with a whisk.
1	Yolk	• Whisk to a smooth paste, then add in the cream.
20g	Plain flour	• Add a couple of tablespoons of the rhubarb liquid into the custard.
50g	Caster sugar	• Arrange the rhubarb into the baked tart.
300ml	Single cream	• Pour the custard mix over the rhubarb.
		• Bake for about 20 minutes.

Topping		Group D
50g	Demerara sugar	• Mix together the oats, demerara sugar, and ginger.
50g	Porridge oats	• Add the melted butter to form the crumble.
50g	Melted butter	• After 20 minutes, remove the flan from the oven. It will still have a slight wobble – that's ok.
30g	Finely chopped crystallised ginger	• Sprinkle the crumble mix on top of the flan.
		• Return to the oven for a further 15 minutes.
		• Remove from the oven to cool.
		• This flan can be served warm with crème fraiche, cream, or ice cream. It can also be served chilled.

Apricot Jane's
Hints and Tips

• Rhubarb is at its best from March to May. I love to go into my garden and freshly pick my champagne rhubarb; the lovely red stems are succulent and shiny. To prepare, first take away the green leaf, which is poisonous; then trim the base and rinse the stem before cutting it into 3cm (1") pieces.

• Ginger goes so well with rhubarb; you could use dried ginger powder, but I like the texture you get with the crystallized ginger.

- The demerara sugar helps to give the crumble a crunch. The oat crumble makes a change from the traditional crumble. Almonds also work well with rhubarb.

- The sharpness of the rhubarb cuts through the sweetness of the custard and pastry.

- If this tart is going to be made in advance, you can brush over the pastry case with a beaten egg. This acts as a barrier to stop the pastry from going soft.

Sesame and Poppy Seed Sharing Loaf

This is a soft dough, easily separated into portions – great for parties. It goes well with cheese and pickles or a homemade soup.

Equipment:	Scales, measuring spoons, scraper, sharp knife, bowl, jug, baking tray 30 x 20cm (12 x 8"), water sprayer, parchment, damp cloth or cling film, plastic sheet, ruler.
Oven:	Pre-heat to 200°C, 190°C fan (420°F); Gas 6.

Dough A / Group A

Dough A		Group A
325g	Strong white flour	• Rub the butter into the flour.
10g (¾ tsp)	Salt	• Add the salt, caster sugar, and dried yeast.
35g	Butter	• Make a well in the centre.
3g (½ tsp)	Caster sugar	
7g (1 sachet)	Dried yeast	

Dough B / Group B

Dough B		Group B
50g	Egg	• Add the whole egg into the well.
20ml	Milk	• Add warm water.
120ml	Water +/-	• Work the flour into the centre to absorb the liquid.
		• Knead the dough for about 10 minutes. This develops the gluten network and creates a smooth elastic dough.
		• Place in a bowl and cover with a damp cloth or cling film and leave in a warm place (26°C or 78°F) to prove for 1 hour until double in size.
		• After the one-hour proving from Group B, knock back the dough.
		• Prove again for a further 30 minutes.
		• See Hints and Tips below.

- Hand mould into a round ball and rest for 10 minutes.

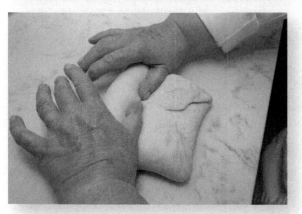

- Flatten slightly, creating a rectangle shape.
- Bring the two ends into the middle.
- Then tuck the top over firmly.

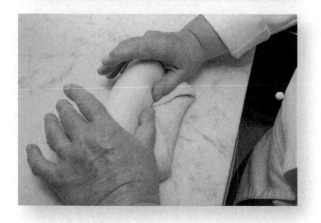

- Take the top of the dough and pinch, bringing it forward, pulling lightly without tearing the dough, and working the dough forward to form a cylinder shape.
- The length should be about 27cm (11″).

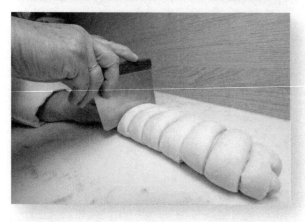

- Take a scraper or a sharp kitchen knife and cut 2cm (¾″) deep straight cuts.

Topping		Group C
40g	Sesame seeds	• Blend the seeds together.
10g	Poppy seeds	

Final Process

- Lightly spray the top with water.
- Carefully roll the top of the dough in the sesame and poppy seed mix.
- Place on the baking tray (either greased or on parchment). Cover with a plastic sheet.
- Prove for about 30 minutes.
- Bake for 20 to 25 minutes.

Apricot Jane's

Hints and Tips

- Dough temperature is important to achieve the best results. The yeast works best at 26° C. This is explained fully in the Section on Bread on page 15.

- As this dough has milk, sugar, butter, and egg, the texture is nice and soft.

- This recipe is also good for making baps.

- Weigh the dough into 70g pieces. (for a yield of 8 baps).

- Mould into round balls and rest the dough.
  - With a rolling pin, roll out the dough balls to 7cm (3") in diameter.
  - These can be left plain, dusted in flour, or water washed and dipped in sesame seeds.
  - Prove until double the size.
  - Bake at the same temperature but for 10 to 12 minutes.

- Note the +/- by the water. This is to indicate that you may need more water or less depending on the quality and strength of the flour.

Shortbread Valentine Biscuits

Shortbread is so popular – you can design so many biscuits from the base recipe. This one has been made for Valentine's Day; a jammy delight.

Equipment:	Scales, measuring spoons, bowl, scraper, heart shape cutter 7 x 5cm (2½ x 2") for the base and top, heart shape cutter 3 x 2.5cm (1½ x 1") for the small heart centre, baking tray 30 x 20cm (12 x 8"), rolling pin, sieve.
Oven:	Pre-heat to 180°C, 170°C fan (350°F); Gas 4.
Yield:	12 biscuits.

Shortbread — Group A

150g	Softened butter	• Cream the softened butter and caster sugar until light and creamy.
75g	Caster sugar	

Group B

150g	Plain flour	• Sieve the flour and cornflour together.
75g	Cornflour	• Add to the creamed mixture and mix to form a paste.
		• Wrap in cling film and rest in the fridge for 15 minutes.

Process

- Roll out the shortbread from Group B to 3mm thick.
- Cut out the heart bases and place them on the baking tray.
- Using the same cutter, cut out the heart tops and cut a smaller heart out of each centre.
- Arrange the hearts on separate trays as the one with the centre taken out will bake in less time.
- Rest the shortbread in the fridge for about 10 minutes before baking.
- Bake for 10 minutes for the bases and 8 minutes for the tops.

Finish

60g	Seedless raspberry jam	• Soften the jam and place it in a piping bag.
		• Pipe a little jam around the edge of each base heart.
25g	Icing sugar	• Using a sieve, lightly dust the top heart with icing sugar.
		• Then gently place the top heart on top of the base heart.
		• Then pipe the jam into the centre of the heart to finish.

- Always use butter for shortbread. Do not use light butter spreads - because of their low-fat content, the shortbread will flow.

- The cornflour helps to shorten the shortbread further as it contains no gluten.

- This recipe could be used for plain shortbread biscuits and fingers. These may need the paste to be a bit thicker. Dust with caster sugar on removal from the oven.

- There is a template for the hearts at the back of this book. See the Section on Templates on page 195.

Simnel Cake

This lovely fruit cake with marzipan baked in the middle and marzipan to finish was a popular Mothering Sunday cake. The girls in service would bring one home for their mothers. Although today we associate it more with Easter.

Equipment: Scales, measuring spoons, mixing bowl, beater, 18cm (7") cake tin, parchment paper, spatula, bowls, blow torch (see Hints and Tips).

Oven: Pre-heat to 150°C, 140°C fan (325°F); Gas 3.

Cake batter 1		Group A
225g	Softened butter	• Cream together the softened butter and sugar until soft and creamy and paler in colour; this takes about 8 minutes.
225g	Light muscovado sugar	• Scrape down the bowl before adding the egg.

Cake batter 2		Group B
225g (4)	Eggs	• Add the egg in about 4 stages, thoroughly mixing each time.
2g	Vanilla	• Always scrape down the sides of the bowl between additions; this is to ensure an even distribution of ingredients.

Cake batter 3		Group C
225g	Plain flour	• Sieve the flour and spice together.
2tsp	Mixed spice	• Fold the flour and spice into the creamed batter.

		Group D
225g	Sultanas	• Add the fruit into the batter using a spatula.
50g	Chopped mixed peel	• Mix to ensure the fruit is evenly distributed.
100g	Glacé cherries	
1 lemon	Zest and juice	

Filling		Group E
200g	Marzipan	• Roll out the 200g of marzipan into a 16cm (6") disc, ready for the next stage.

Assembly

- Line the cake tin with parchment paper.
- Deposit 300g of cake mixture into the lined cake tin.
- Level the mixture.
- Place the 200g marzipan disc on top of the fruit cake mix.
- Add the remainder of the cake mix on top of the marzipan and level the surface.
- Bake for about 2 hours.
- Remove from the oven and leave in the tin to go cold.

Finishing

150g	Marzipan
50g	Apricot Jam
1	Egg

- Roll out 150g of marzipan to 4mm thick, sufficient to cover the top of the cake.
- Boil the apricot jam and brush over the top of the fruit cake.
- Place the marzipan on top of the fruit cake.
- Divide the remaining marzipan into 11 balls. You can score the top of the marzipan with a design before brushing it over with the egg.
- Beat the egg and brush it over the surface of the marzipan.
- Evenly place the 11 marzipan balls around the top and lightly brush with the egg.
- With a blow torch, toast the marzipan top and balls.

Apricot Jane's Hints and Tips

- When I take the cake out of the oven, I cover the top with parchment paper and then place a baking tray on top to trap the steam. This softens the crumb and keeps the cake nice and moist.

- When placing the disc of marzipan in the middle of the cake, I always leave a 1.5cm (1/2") edge because the marzipan will spread a bit in baking.

- If you do not have a blow torch, you can put the cake in a hot oven or use the grill in the oven to toast the marzipan.

- You could pop a chick in the centre of the cake with some mini eggs if it's for Easter. For Mother's Day, you could decorate it with some sugar flowers.

Sweet Chilli Salmon Tarts

A crisp pastry tart that is great for a light lunch and served with salad.

Equipment: Scales, measuring spoons, mixing bowl, 6 x 8cm (3") round fluted tins, baking tray, whisk, baking beans.
Oven: Pre-heat to 180°C, 170°C fan (350°F); Gas 6.
Yield: 6 tarts.

Pastry stage 1 — Group A

100g	Plain flour	• Rub the butter into the flour and polenta.
30g	Polenta	• Then add the parmesan.
75g	Salted butter	• Blend together.
15g	Finely grated parmesan	

Pastry stage 2 — Group B

| 2 tbsp | Cold water | • Add the cold water to the dry ingredients of Group A and bind them together to form a paste. |
| | | • Wrap in cling film and chill for 20 minutes. |

Process

- Spray grease the flan tins.
- Roll out the pastry to have a 3mm thickness and line each case.
- Prepare the cases for blind baking (See the Section on Shortcrust and Sweet Pastry on page 33 for blind baking).
- Chill for 20 minutes.
- Bake for 15 minutes.
- Remove the bakingbeans and continue baking to dry out the case – about five minutes.

Filling stage 1 — Group C

120g	Salmon	• Place the salmon pieces on foil and put the sweet chilli sauce on top of the salmon.
2 tbsp	Sweet chilli sauce	• Wrap the salmon in the foil.
		• Bake for 20 minutes.
		• Remove and allow to go cold.

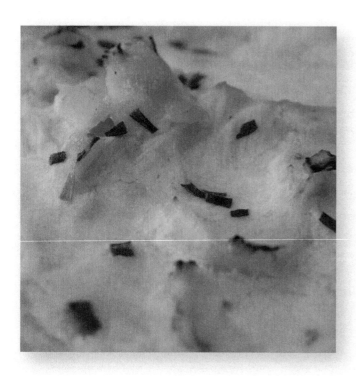

Filling stage 2 — Group D

2tbsp	Chopped chives	
2	Eggs	
140ml	Whipping cream	
2 tbsp	Sweet chilli sauce from salmon	
Seasoning	Salt and pepper	

- Mix the eggs and cream together.
- Add the chives.
- Add the chilli sauce juice from the baked salmon.
- Season with salt and pepper.
- Flake the salmon and divide it between the tartlets.
- Pour over the filling mix.
- Bake for about 20 minutes until set.

Apricot Jane's Hints and Tips

- Polenta is coarsely ground corn. It is gluten free and is high in complex carbs, so it keeps you full for longer.

- The pastry for this product is nice and crisp, and the polenta gives a good colour. It makes a change from shortcrust pastry because of the texture. It works well as a case for a wide range of fillings.

Tomato, Herb, and Garlic Focaccia

Delicious dipped in balsamic vinegar and olive oil, with cold meats and cheese, or it can be eaten as part of a full meal or as a sandwich.

Equipment:	Scales, measuring spoons, mixer with a dough hook, mixing bowl for the pre-ferment, jug for oil infusion, sharp knife, plastic scraper, rolling pin, baking tray 30 x 20cm (12 x 8").
Oven:	Pre-heat to 220°C, 210°C fan (425°F); Gas 7.
Dough temperature:	26°C (78°F). See Hints and Tips.

Pre-ferment | Group A

100g	Strong flour
2g (½ tsp)	Dried yeast
3g (½ tsp)	Salt
100ml	Water

- Mix all ingredients together to form a dough.
- There is no need to develop the dough – cover over with cling film and leave it in the fridge overnight.

Oil infusion | Group B

30ml	Olive oil
10g	Garlic

- Infuse the peeled and crushed garlic in the oil.
- Leave overnight.

Dough | Group C

280g	Strong flour
200g	Wholemeal flour
9g (1 tbsp)	Salt
7g (1 sachet)	Dried yeast
15g (1 tbsp)	Dried mixed herbs
267g (all)	Pre-ferment
320g	Warm water
15g (1 tbsp)	Tomato puree
30g	Finely chopped sundried tomato

- Mix the tomato puree and half of the oil infusion together. Keep the remainder of the oil infusion until the end – see Processing.
- Place flour, salt, herbs, and dried yeast into the mixing bowl and just blend together
- Add the oil, tomato puree, and water and blend with the pre-ferment to form a dough either in a mixer with a dough hook (mix for 10 minutes) or:
- by hand, work the dough by kneading to develop the gluten network. It will take about 10 minutes to create a smooth elastic dough. Use oiled hands if the dough is sticky.
- Place the dough in a bowl and cover with a damp cloth or cling film and leave to prove for 1 hour in a warm place.
- After 1 hour, knock back the dough and add the sundried tomatoes.
- Cover again and prove for another 30 minutes.

Processing

- Lightly oil the baking tray.
- Remove the dough from the bowl.
- Gently stretch the dough to fit the baking tray to about 2cm (½") deep.
- Allow to prove for about 15 minutes.
- Oil your fingers and then press across the dough to create mini dips.

- Place thinly sliced tomatoes on top (Group D).
- Drizzle over the remaining garlic-infused olive oil.
- Final prove for about 20 minutes.
- Bake for 25 minutes.

Topping		Group D
2	Large tomatoes	• Infuse the oil and garlic together.
5g	Rock salt	• Thinly slice the tomatoes.
		• Sprinkle the top with rock salt.

Apricot Jane's Hints and Tips

- Dough temperature is important to achieve the best results. The yeast works best at 26°C. This is explained fully in the Section on Bread on page 15.

- If you want a plain focaccia, then omit the garlic and tomato paste and wholemeal flour.

- You can also add other inclusions, e.g., chopped olives, basil, and onions topped with mozzarella cheese, garlic, and fresh rosemary.

- Olive oil, as well as being healthier, helps to give a good flavour. It also develops the elasticity of the dough.

- The more hydration you give the dough, the more open the structure. If the dough is soft, oil your hands when handling it.

SUMMER

The long hazy days of Summer,
A time to relax and enjoy
the beauty of nature,
A chance to recharge and just be.

A collection of seasonal recipes
to make, bake, and enjoy
with friends.

Banana, Date, and Walnut Loaf Cake

A great recipe for using up ripe bananas; a lovely moist cake for afternoon tea.

Equipment:	Scales, measuring spoons, mixer with a beater attachment, bowls, spatula, 1kg (2lb) loaf tin, fine needle cake tester.
Oven:	Pre-heat to 175°C, 165°C fan (375°F); Gas 4.

Group A

300g	Ripe bananas	• Peel and chop the bananas.

Cake batter — Group B

100g	Butter	• Cream the butter and sugar together until light and creamy.
200g	Light brown sugar	• Add the eggs in two stages, beating well between each addition.
2	Eggs	• Add the vanilla.
2.5g (½ tsp)	Vanilla	• Add the chopped bananas from Group A and mix together.

Group C

180g	Plain flour	• Sieve all the dry ingredients together.
5g (1 tsp)	Baking powder	• Using a spatula, add the dry ingredients into the creamed banana batter.
2.5g (½ tsp)	Bicarbonate of soda	• Mix to a clear consistency so that there are no signs of the flour.
5g (1 tsp)	Cinnamon	

Filling — Group D

80g	Chopped dates	• Grease and flour the loaf tin.
80g	Chopped walnuts	• Using a spatula add the dates, walnuts, and pumpkin seeds into the banana batter.
20g	Pumpkin seeds	• Mix until all the filling ingredients are covered in the batter.
		• Deposit the whole mixture into the prepared loaf tin.
		• Level the top.

Topping		Group E
10g	Chopped walnuts	• Sprinkle the top with walnuts, pumpkin seeds, and nib sugar.
5g	Pumpkin seeds	• Bake for 60 minutes.
5g	Nib sugar	• To check if the loaf is baked, push the needle cake tester into the middle, and it should come out clean.

• Always use overripe bananas for best results because, as the banana ages, it becomes sweeter and makes a moister cake.

• You can adjust this recipe and change the dates for chocolate chips, and then you could sprinkle chocolate chips on top of the cake.

• Of course, you can cut out the nuts and dates and keep it absolutely plain, but the addition of nuts gives an interesting texture.

Chocolate Chip Cookies

These chocolate chip cookies have a great texture.

Equipment:	Scales, measuring spoons, bowl, spatula, 30 x 20cm (12 x 8") baking tray, parchment paper, cooling wire, palette knife.
Oven:	Pre-heat to 180°C, 165°C fan (350°F); Gas 4.
Yield:	12 cookies.

Group A

75g	Softened butter	• Cream together the softened butter, granulated sugar, and soft brown sugar until light and creamy.
40g	Light soft brown sugar	
40g	Granulated sugar	

Group B

40g (1)	Egg	• Add the egg into the creamed batter and mix until clear.
25g	Lemon juice	• Add the lemon juice and vanilla and blend together.
2g (½ tsp)	Vanilla	

Group C

110g	Plain flour	• Sieve the flour, baking powder, cinnamon, and salt.
2g (½ tsp)	Baking powder	• Fold into the batter (Groups A + B) and mix together.
1g (¼ tsp)	Cinnamon	
1g (¼ tsp)	Sea salt	

Group D

170g	Chocolate chips	• Line the baking tray with parchment paper.
65g	Chopped walnuts	• Add the chocolate chips, walnuts, and oats into the batter and mix to ensure they are evenly dispersed.
20g	Rolled oats	• Deposit 50g of mix and place on the baking tray, allowing space for the cookie to flow a little.
		• Bake for approximately 12-15 minutes.
		• Remove from the tray when cooled, as they will be fragile when hot.

- The beauty of this recipe is you can adapt it to your own flavour palate.

- The chocolate can be dark, milk, or white. A mix can be used if you like.

- The walnuts could be exchanged for hazelnut, pecans, or pistachios.

Coconut Macaroons Dipped in Chocolate

A soft, chewy coconut macaroon dipped in chocolate gives a great energy boost with afternoon tea.

Equipment: Scales, measuring spoons, mixer with whisk attachment, bowl, piping bag, piping tube 3mm plain, baking tray 30 x 20cm (12 x 8″), silicone mat or parchment (either can be used), thermometer.

Oven: Pre-heat to 150°C, 140°C fan (300°F); Gas 2.

Yield: 28 macaroons.

Meringue		Group A
2	Egg whites	• Using a sterile bowl and whisk, place the egg whites in the bowl and whisk to a soft peak.
100g	Caster sugar	• Gradually add the sugar; continue whisking to dissolve the sugar and to achieve stiff peak consistency.

		Group B
30g	Plain flour	• Mix the coconut and flour together.
120g	Desiccated coconut	• Using a spatula, fold in the vanilla.
½ tsp	Vanilla	• Then fold in the coconut and flour mix in three stages, being careful to maintain the volume.

Topping		Group C
7	Glacé cherries	• Place the meringue into a piping bag with the tube.
		• Pipe bulbs 4cm (1½″) in diameter.
		• Cut each of the cherries into four and place a cherry quarter on top of each bulb in the middle.
		• Bake for 20 to 25 minutes.
		• When baked, the coconut macaroon should lift off the silicone mat without sticking.

Finishing		Group D
100g	Dark chocolate couverture	• Temper the chocolate as explained in Hints and Tips.
		• When the coconut macaroons are cold, dip the base into the chocolate.
		• Clear the base from drips and place it onto the parchment to set.

- To temper the chocolate:
  - Melt it to 45°C;
  - Reduce the temperature to 27°C then:
  - Heat the chocolate to 31°C.

- There is more on chocolate and how it behaves in the Section on Ingredient functions on page 5.

- If you prefer, you can use cooking chocolate which doesn't need to be tempered in this way.

- Using a dark chocolate couverture complements the meringue's sweetness, but milk or white chocolate could be used if desired.

- These macaroons could be piped larger to 6cm in diameter but piped in a ring.

English Madeleines

I was invited to Tokyo, Japan, to make an afternoon tea with English baking. One of the products I chose was the English madeleine. Everyone fell in love with this delicious cake; perfect for afternoon tea.

Equipment:	Scales, measuring spoons, mixer, beater attachment, scraper, dariole moulds, 1.5cm piping tube, piping bag, pastry brush, saucepan, bowl.
Oven:	Pre-heat to 170°C, 160°C fan (325°F); Gas 4.
Yield:	About 14 Madeleines.

Group A

150g	Softened butter	• Cream together the butter and sugar until light and creamy.
150g	Caster sugar	

Group B

150g (3)	Eggs	• Mix the eggs and vanilla together.
3g	Vanilla	• Add the eggs a little at a time, scraping down the bowl between additions.

Group C

115g	Plain flour	• Blend the flour, almonds, and baking powder together.
40g	Ground almonds	• Fold all the dry ingredients into the batter.
5g	Baking powder	• If needed, add a tablespoon of milk to ensure a dropping consistency.

Process

- Grease and flour the dariole moulds.
- Place the mixture into a piping bag with a plain tube of 1.5cm.
- Pipe into the dariole moulds to ¾ full.
- Bake for 20 to 25 minutes. The sponge will spring back when baked.
- Remove from the oven and allow to cool; then ease the sponges from the moulds.

Topping — Group D

150g	Red jam	• Boil the jam with a little water.
150g	Desiccated coconut	• Brush the jam onto the sponge.
		• Roll in the desiccated coconut until all covered.

Group E

75g	Unsalted butter
75g	Icing sugar
3g	Vanilla
7	Glacé cherries

- Cream together the softened butter, icing sugar, and vanilla until creamy.
- Place in a piping bag with a 1.5cm plain tube.
- Pipe a rosette on top of each Madeleine and then place ½ cherry on the top.

Apricot Jane's
Hints and Tips

- If you don't have dariole moulds, you can bake these in cupcake cases and remove the wrapper for finishing.

- I grease the mould by brushing with melted shortening, then lightly dust with flour.

- Leave the Madeleines to cool a little before removing them from the mould (if using cupcake cases, allow to go cold before removing the paper).

Feta Cheese, Honey, and Sesame Tarts with Pita Bread

A great lunch, sitting under my grapevine at home. The sun is shining, and lunch is served with a glass of crisp white wine.

Equipment:	Scales, measuring spoons, mixing bowl, 7 x 7cm (3") square tartlet tins, baking tray 30 x 20cm (12 x 8"), bowl, whisk, baking beans, stone for pita bread.
Oven:	Pre-heat to 180°C, 170°C fan (350°F); Gas 4 for the pastry and filling. Pita bread: Adjust the oven to 220°C, 200°C fan (425°F); Gas 6.
Yield:	6 tarts, 4 pita breads.

Pastry

Group A

100g	Plain flour	• Mix the flour and polenta together.
30g	Polenta	• Rub the butter into the flour mix.
75g	Salted butter	• Add the parmesan.
15g	Finely grated parmesan	• Blend together.

Group B

2 tbsp	Cold water	• Add the cold water to the dry ingredients from Group A and bind them together to form a paste.
		• Wrap in cling film and chill for 20 minutes.

Process

- Grease the flan tins.
- Roll out the pastry to 3m (⅓") thick and line each case.
- Line with greaseproof paper and fill with baking beans (See Hints and Tips for blind baking).
- Chill for 20 minutes.
- Blind bake for 15 minutes (180°C, 170°C fan).
- Remove the baking beans and continue baking to dry out the case.

Filling		Group C
150g	Feta cheese	• Slice the feta cheese, allowing 25g per tartlet case.
90g	Runny honey	• Place the honey, olive oil, and roasted sesame seeds together in a bowl and warm in the oven for 5 minutes – this makes pouring evenly over the feta cheese easier.
15ml	Olive oil	
40g	Roasted sesame seeds	• Just before pouring over the tartlets, add the chives or oregano.
2 tbsp	Chopped chives or oregano	• Bake for 15 minutes (180°C, 170°C fan).

Pita bread		Group D
250g	Strong flour	• Place all dry ingredients into a bowl.
5g (1 tsp)	Salt	• Add the warm water and oil and mix the dough to develop the gluten.
8g	Dried yeast	• Cover the dough and prove for 45 minutes.
150ml	Warm water	• Divide the dough into 4 x 100g pieces.
15g (1 tbsp)	Olive oil	• Mould into balls and rest.
5g	Chopped chives	• Using a rolling pin, roll out the dough into an oblong shape 5mm thick.
		• To get the best result, place either a baking tray in the oven to get hot or use a stone.
		• Place the pitas directly onto the stone or tray. The pitas will puff up.
		• Bake for 15 minutes (220°C, 200°C fan).

Apricot Jane's Hints and Tips

• Baking the tartlet blind is important because it only takes 15 minutes to bake, and the case should be nice and crisp (see the section on Shortcrust and Sweet Pastry on page 33 for blind baking).

• Baking the pita bread on a stone or hot tray helps to give a lift to the dough and create a hollow centre.

• Roasting the sesame seeds develops more flavour for the tartlet.

• Lovely for lunch served with a Greek salad of red pepper, vine tomatoes, feta cheese cubes, and olives drizzled in virgin olive oil and warm pita bread

Flap Jacks with Orange and Sultanas

This recipe was always a popular one in our student bakery shop, always selling out. Great for lunch boxes and picnics and a good energy food.

Equipment:	Scales, measuring spoons, saucepan, spatula, bowl, 20 muffin tins (or baking tray 30 x 20cm (12 x 8").
Oven:	Pre-heat to 180°C, 170°C fan (350°F); Gas 4.
Yield:	20 flap jacks at 50g.

Group A

250g	Butter	• Place the butter, syrup, and sugar into a saucepan.
225g	Golden syrup	• Heat gently to melt the butter and dissolve the sugar and bring to a boil.
75g	Light brown sugar	• Remove from the heat.

Group B

375g	Oats	• Add the juice to the saucepan with the butter syrup from Group A.
120g	Sultanas	• Place the oats, sultanas, and zest of orange in a bowl.
1	Zest and juice of an orange	• Pour the syrup into the oats and stir until the mixture has all been moistened.
		• Grease and line the bases of the muffin tins or the base of the baking tray.
		• Put 50g of the mixture into each muffin tin or place all the mixture into the baking tray for the slab.
		• Bake for 13 minutes in the muffin tins or 20 minutes for the slab.

Group C

100g	Couverture chocolate	• Temper the chocolate as explained in Hints and Tips.
		• Place the chocolate in a piping bag.
		• Spin the chocolate over each flap jack to complete.

- To temper the chocolate:
  - Melt it to 45°C;
  - Reduce the temperature to 27°C then:
  - Heat the chocolate to 31°C.

There is more on chocolate and how it behaves in the section on Ingredient Functions on page 5.

- If you prefer, you can use cooking chocolate which doesn't need to be tempered in this way.

- This flapjack recipe can be adapted in so many ways. I thought I would try baking them in muffin tins for a change, but this mix could be baked in a slab tin 30 x 20cm (12 x 8"), then you can cut the flapjacks into fingers or squares.

- To change textures and flavours, consider nuts, coconut, chocolate chips, cherries, apricots, or cranberries.

Frangipane Tartlets

These tartlets have a lovely butter crisp pastry and a moist frangipane filling. I have suggested a variety of toppings to enjoy.

Equipment:	Scales, measuring spoons, mixer with a beater attachment, bowls, baking trays, scraper, 1cm plain piping tube, piping bag, zest grater, tartlet tray with 12 sections, 7cm (3") round cutter, rolling pin, cooling wire, spatula, saucepan, pastry brush.
Oven:	Pre-heat to 175°C, 160°C fan (350°F); Gas 4.
Yield:	12 tartlets with different toppings.

Pastry — Group A

250g	Plain flour	• Mix the sugar and egg together with the zest of the lemon.
135g	Butter	• Rub the fat into the flour.
32g (1)	Egg	• Add the sugar, egg, and zest into the flour and bring together to form a paste.
62g	Caster sugar	• Wrap in cling film and place in the fridge to rest.
1	Zest of lemon	

Frangipane filling — Group B

100g	Caster sugar	• Cream the butter and sugar together until light and creamy.
100g	Butter	• Then add the egg in stages beating well between additions.
100g (3)	Eggs	• Fold in the flour, ground almonds, and orange zest to form a batter.
50g	Plain flour	
50g	Ground almonds	
1 zest	Orange	

Pastry Process — Group C

50g	Red jam	• Take the pastry (Group A) from the fridge; roll out the pastry thinly to about 3mm (¼") thick.
		• Using the 7cm round cutter, cut out the discs.
		• Place the discs into the lightly greased tartlet tins; press around the edges to ensure there are no air bubbles.
		• Place the red jam into a piping bag and pipe a spot in the centre of the base of each tartlet.

Filling and Baking — Group D

20g	Flaked almonds	• Place the frangipane into the piping bag with the 1cm plain piping tube.
15g	Blueberries	• Holding the bag upright, pipe directly over the red jam – push evenly to fill the tartlet ¾ full.
15g	Raspberries	• For the 12 tartlets:

- Place the frangipane into the piping bag with the 1cm plain piping tube.
- Holding the bag upright, pipe directly over the red jam – push evenly to fill the tartlet ¾ full.
- For the 12 tartlets:
  - sprinkle 3 tartlets with flaked almonds,
  - sprinkle 3 tartlets with blueberries,
  - sprinkle 3 tartlets with raspberries,
- leave the remaining 3 tartlets plain.
- Bake all the tartlets for 25 minutes.
- After baking, remove the tartlets from the baking tray to a cooling wire.

Post-bake toppings — Group E

80g	Smooth apricot jam
1 tbsp	Water
2 tbsp	Lemon juice
100g	Icing sugar
3	Glacé cherries

- Place the apricot jam and water together in a saucepan and bring to a boil.
- Using a pastry brush, evenly coat the apricot jam on top of all the baked frangipane tartlets.
- Mix the icing sugar and lemon juice together (The correct consistency is when the icing is dropped, it finds its own level).
  - Flaked almond tartlets:
    Gently brush the icing over the tartlets so the almonds just show through and the topping is thin.
  - Raspberry tartlets:
    Brush the icing over the frangipane.
  - Blueberry tartlets:
    Leave without any icing.
  - Plain tartlets:
    Add more icing to the mix to thicken it enough to cover the top of the tartlets, then place a cherry on the top.

Apricot Jane's
Hints and Tips

- Frangipane tarts can be made in a large flan 20cm (8").

- Other fruits that can be used are apricots, rhubarb, apple, or plum.

- The apricot glaze will help keep the fruits looking fresh and keep the tartlets from drying out.

- Delicious served warm with crème fresh, cream, or ice cream.

Garlic and Cheese Swirl

This is a great tear and share bread. It can be served at a buffet for lunch with a cheese board or with soup.

Equipment: Scales, measuring spoons, scraper, bowl, rolling pin, grater, knife, frame: (either 18cm (7") hoop or cake tin or foil), parchment paper, ruler, cooling wire, cling film or a damp cloth.

Oven: Pre-heat to 210°C, 200°C fan (465°F); Gas 6.

Dough temperature: 26°C (78°F). See Hints and Tips.

Dough stage 1 — Group A

200g	Strong flour	• Rub the butter into the flour.
3g (½ tsp)	Salt	• Blend in the salt, sugar, and dried yeast.
15g	Butter	• Make a well in the centre.
10g	Sugar	
5g (1 tsp)	Dried yeast	

Dough stage 2 — Group B

75ml	Milk	• Place the egg in the well.
50g (1)	Egg	• Add in the warm milk.
5g	Chopped parsley and chives	• Using one hand, draw the ingredients together and knead to develop the dough for about 10 minutes until the dough is smooth and elastic.
		• Place the dough in a bowl, cover with cling film and leave to prove for 1 hour in a warm place.
		• Knock back the dough and add the chopped parsley and chives.
		• Allow it to rest for 15 minutes.

Filling — Group C

25g	Butter or Philadelphia cream cheese	• Roll out the dough on a lightly floured surface to 28 x 15cm (11 x 6").
		• I use Philadelphia cream cheese and chives and add extra garlic and chopped parsley and chives, so you can choose between butter or the cheese. Spread the cream cheese over the rolled-out dough.
5g (1 tsp)	Garlic paste	
3g (½ tsp)	Chopped parsley and chives	• Sprinkle with 20g of grated cheese.
20g	Grated cheese	• Roll up the dough from the top towards yourself. Pull the dough very slightly as you roll, so it is firm. The length should be 28cm (11").
		• Mark out 4cm (1.5") so the dough is divided into 7 pieces, then cut through.
		• Arrange the dough pieces into the greased hoop, one in the centre and the remainder around.
		• Prove the dough until double its size – about 30 minutes.

Topping	Group D	
20g	Grated cheese	• After proving, sprinkle the top with the grated cheese.
		• Bake for 25 minutes.
		• Remove from the oven.
		• When cool, remove the frame. If in a sealed tin, remove it as soon as you can to avoid the base sweating.

Apricot Jane's
Hints and Tips

• Dough temperature is important to achieve the best results. The yeast works best at 26°C. This is explained fully in the Section on Bread on page 15.

• This recipe can be adapted to suit your palate. Here are some suggestions:

  - Pesto paste (25g) spread on the dough with the 25g grated cheese,

  - Chopped olives (20g) and feta cheese (25g) or oregano (1/2 tsp).

Rose Pavlova

This pavlova, with its hint of pink and the rose flavour, complemented with the raspberry, was my reflection of the English rose for the afternoon tea in Tokyo, Japan.

Equipment:	Scales, measuring spoons, mixer with a whisk attachment, spatula, piping bag, star tube, baking tray with either a silicone mat or parchment.
Oven:	Pre-heat to 120°C, 110°C fan (275°F); Gas 1.
Yield:	10 pavlovas.

Group A

90g (3)	Egg white	• Using a sterilised bowl and whisk, beat the egg whites with 50g of the caster sugar until thick and white.
180g	Caster sugar	• Gradually add the remaining caster sugar until it has all been absorbed into the whites and a stiff peak is achieved.

Group B

1tsp	Corn flour	• Blend the corn flour, white wine vinegar, rose water, and colouring together.
½ tsp	White wine vinegar	• Add to the meringue at a slow speed.
½ tsp	Rose water	• Place the meringue into a piping bag with the star tube.
¼ tsp	Pink colouring	

Process

- On one side of the parchment paper, draw 7 pencil circles 7cm (3") in diameter, leaving 5cm (2") between circles. Turn the parchment over — the circles will then be visible to act as your template.
- Pipe the meringue from the centre of each circle to the outside edge — one layer.
- Pipe 7-9 small bulbs on the top edge of each circle around the edge to create a nest.
- Bake for about 45-60 minutes.
- When baked, the pavlova will lift off the paper.

Topping — Group C

125ml	Whipping cream	• Place the cream in a bowl, and using a whisk, whip to soft peak consistency.
1 tsp	Vanilla	• Add the vanilla, rose water, and sugar.
1 tsp	Rose water	• Whip a little more until you can pipe the cream without it collapsing.
20g	Caster sugar	

Assemble

250g	Raspberries	• Place the cream in a piping bag with the star tube and pipe a rosette of cream boldly on the top of the meringue.
25g	Blueberries	

• Arrange the raspberries and blueberries on top. Cut some in half longways to show the juicy interior of the raspberry and blueberry.

Apricot Jane's
Hints and Tips

- Sterilising the whisk and bowl in boiling water removes all traces of grease. This is important and is explained in the Section on Meringues on page 43.

- The first addition of sugar will help stabilise the meringue.

- Adding the remainder of the sugar slowly stops the meringue from collapsing.

- The corn flour helps with the chewiness of the centre of the pavlova.

- A pre-heated oven helps to set the meringue quickly so it does not collapse.

- If you like, you could change the flavours, colours, and fruit topping.

- This pavlova could be piped as one large 23cm (9") base.

- The pavlova keeps well in an airtight tin.

White Cob Using Pre-Ferment Sponge

The flavour developed by the pre-ferment is worth doing. A crusty cob goes so well with cheese, soup, butter, and a good jam.

Equipment:	Scales, measuring spoons, dough thermometer, scraper, sieve, sharp serrated dough knife (or blade), bowl, oiled plastic sheet or cling film, baking tray 30 x 20cm (12 x 8").
Oven:	Pre-heat to 220°C, 210°C fan (425°F); Gas 7. Place a bowl of water in the oven to create steam.
Dough temperature:	26°C (78°F). See Hints and Tips.

Pre-ferment sponge — Group A

230g	Strong white flour	• Mix the flour, yeast, and water together. There is no need to develop this dough.
2g (½ tsp)	Dried yeast	• Cover the dough over an oiled plastic sheet and leave it to ferment for 8 to 24 hours ambient for a minimum of 8 hours, but overnight and up to 24 hours is fine.
120g	Water (cold)	

Main dough — Group B

230g	Strong white flour	• Rub the shortening into the flour.
15g	Shortening	• Add the remaining dry ingredients and make a well in the centre.
7g (¾ tsp)	Salt	• Pour half the water into the well. By hand, start drawing in the flour, using a scraper to gather up the flour.
12g (1 tbsp)	Sugar	• Then place all the sponge from Group A in the centre and add the remaining water.
5g (¾ tbsp)	Milk powder	• Gather up the rest of the flour and work the dough together by kneading for at least 10 minutes until the dough is smooth and elastic.
7g (1 sachet)	Dried yeast	
140ml	Warm water	• Cover over with an oiled plastic sheet or cling film and leave to prove for 1 hour in a warm place.

Process

- After 1 hour, knock back the dough to equalise the dough temperature.
- Cover and leave for a further 30 minutes.
- Hand mould the dough to express the gases; leave to recover (rest) for 10 minutes.

Topping — Group C

20g	flour	• This is for sieving onto the dough surface after proof – see final stage below.

Final stage

- Mould the dough into a firm ball – it should be nice and smooth on top.
- Grease the baking tray.
- Place the dough on the baking tray; cover it with plastic, and prove in a warm place until double the size.
- Using a sieve, lightly dust the dough piece with the flour (Group C).
- Then, with the sharp knife, cut one line down the middle, then three lines evenly spaced on the left. Repeat on the right-hand side. Each cut should be about 2mm deep, just below the skin of the dough. See the picture.
- Place in the prepared oven – see Oven above.
- Bake for 25 minutes.
- When baked, test by tapping the base of the bread – it should sound hollow.
- Remove from the oven and place on a cooling wire.

Apricot Jane's Hints and Tips

- Dough temperature is important to achieve the best results. The yeast works best at 26°C. This is explained fully in the Section on Bread on page 15.

- The pre-ferment will help to impart a good flavour. Note that the full development process described in the Section on Bread on page 15 isn't necessary for the pre-ferment stage.

- This recipe could be used for tin bread, cottage loaf, or Bloomer.

- Always use a sharp knife or a blade to cut the dough to release tension.

- The dough expands in the first stage of baking which we call 'oven spring.' If there is a weak area, it can burst open. Cutting the dough gives a design. It helps the dough to expand a little more, releasing tension and helping to keep a better shape.

- If you want, you can use a mixer with a dough hook attachment.

AUTUMN

A time for nature to let go
of its golden beauty,
The leaves on the trees fall
golden to the ground,
The Earth yields its harvest,
Now it is time to rest.

A collection of seasonal recipes
to make, bake, and bring comfort
on chilly evenings to enjoy
with friends.

Nutty Treacle Tartlets

This recipe has been adapted from a treacle tart. It's more decadent because of the nuts and has a great texture.

Equipment:	Scales, measuring spoons, bowl, whisk, baking tray, tartlet cases 7cm (3") round or 1 long rectangular tin 32 x 7cm (13 x 3"), cling film, baking beans, greaseproof paper.
Oven:	Pre-heat to 180°C 170°C fan 350°F; Gas 4.
Yield:	7 tartlets or one large tart.

Pastry — Group A

175g	Plain flour	• Rub the butter into the flour and add the zest of the lemon.
85g	Butter	• Mix the egg and caster sugar together.
40g	Caster sugar	• Add to the crumble and mix to form a paste.
1	Egg	• Wrap in cling film and place in the fridge for 30 minutes.
1	Zest of lemon	

Process

- Grease the tartlet cases well.
- Roll out the pastry 2mm thick and use it to line the tartlet cases.
- Line with greaseproof paper and fill with baking beans.
- Chill for 10 minutes, then bake blind for 10 minutes. See Hints and Tips for blind baking.
- Remove the beans and bake the tartlets until set.

Filling — Group B

125g	Golden syrup	• Place the golden syrup, juice of lemon, cream, and egg into a bowl and whisk together.
½	Juice of lemon	
35g	Double cream	• Add the breadcrumbs, allowing 10 minutes for the breadcrumbs to absorb the syrup mixture.
1	Egg	
30g	Breadcrumbs	

Topping — Group C

75g	Mixed nuts: pecan, almond, hazelnuts, pistachio	• Lightly roast all the nuts in the oven and cool. • Deposit Group B mixture evenly into the tartlet cases. • Scatter the mixed nuts evenly on top of the filling. • Bake for 20 minutes until set.
30g	Apricot Jam	• Remove from the oven and cool before very lightly brushing the top with boiled apricot jam. This will give a lovely glaze.

Apricot Jane's

Hints and Tips

- Blind Baking is explained in the Section on Shortcrust and Sweet Pastry on page 33.

- This treacle tart is delicious and has a lovely nutty crunch - a little more extravagant than the traditional treacle tart.

- The lemon helps to cut across the sweetness of the syrup.

- The double cream adds richness and the egg helps to set the mixture.

- Lovely served warm with ice cream.

Gingernut Biscuits

A ginger nut – crisp and perfect for dipping in a hot cup of tea.

Equipment:	Scales, measuring spoons, mixing bowl, spatula, baking trays 30 x 20cm (12 x 8"), palate knife, measuring spoons.
Oven:	Pre-heat to 180°C, 170°C fan (350°F); Gas 4.
Yield:	This recipe will give you around 13 biscuits of about 20g each.

Group A

50g	Butter	• Rub the butter into the flour to resemble breadcrumbs.
100g	Plain four	

Group B

50g	Soft brown sugar	• Place all dry ingredients into a bowl.
1 tsp	Baking powder	• Add Group A into the dry ingredients and blend together with a spatula.
1 tsp	Bicarbonate of soda	
7g (1½ tsp)	Ground ginger	
Pinch of	Salt	
Pinch of	Mixed spice	

Group C

55g	Golden syrup	• Warm the golden syrup in the microwave, then add it to the dry ingredients, and with a spatula, stir to a paste.
		• Weigh the dough into 20g pieces.
		• Roll in a ball and place on a baking tray with silicone paper, and slightly flatten the ball. Six on a tray.
		• Bake for about 8 to 10 minutes.

- Leave space between the balls, as this biscuit will flow during baking.

- The top will crack, which is normal - the baking powder and bicarbonate of soda help to give the crack.

- The golden syrup helps with the flow.

- Don't move the biscuits off the tray until set, as they will be too soft - setting will make them crisp.

- They will seem to drop on removal from the oven - this is normal.

Country Grain Cob

A lovely seeded bread – great with cheese or a hearty soup.

Equipment: Scales, measuring spoons, bowl, mixer with dough hook attachment, greased baking tray, dough scraper, water sprayer, cling film or damp cloth.

Oven: Pre-heat to 220°C, 210°C fan (425°F); Gas 7.
Place a tray of water in the oven to create steam.

Dough temperature: 26°C (78°F). See Hints and Tips.

Dough		Group A
500g	Country grain flour	• Rub the butter into the flour.
40g	Butter	

		Group B
10g	Dried yeast	• Add the yeast and salt into the flour.
10g	Salt	

		Group C
½ tsp	Treacle	• Blend the treacle into the water.
300ml	Warm water	• Add this to the dry ingredients and mix to a dough.
		• Knead the dough for about 10 minutes to develop the gluten.
		• Cover with cling film or a damp cloth and prove the dough for one hour at 26°C.

Process

- Knock back the dough, then cover it again for a further 15 minutes.
- Mould into a cob (a round ball) and cover again for five minutes.
- Final mould the cob shape.
- Cover with cling film or a damp cloth and prove for about 30 minutes.
- Ensure the water is in the oven base to create steam (I also lightly spray water in as I place the dough in the oven).
- Bake in the oven for 35-40 minutes.
- After 30 minutes, open the oven door to let the steam out and continue baking.
- To check for baking, tap the base of the cob – it should sound hollow when baking is complete.

• Dough temperature is important to achieve the best results. The yeast works best at 26°C. This is explained fully in the Section on Bread on page 15.

• Treacle is a yeast food and will also add colour to the dough.

• Butter helps to soften the crumb and hold the bubble structure stable.

Apricot Jane's

Hints and Tips

- Prove the dough in a warm place covered with either a damp cloth or cling film. This will help to avoid getting a skin on the dough surface.

- The steam in the oven helps to give a lift to the dough and give a crust and shine to the surface.

- This dough could be placed in a loaf tin or turned into rolls, each weighing about 60g.

- See the Section on Ingredient Functions on page 5 for different types of flour.

Rocky Road Squares

This is an unbaked product but so popular I had to include it for all you chocolate lovers.

Equipment: Scales, bowl, saucepan, spatula, baking tray 30 x 20cm (12 x 8"), parchment paper.
No need to bake.

Group A

150g	Dark chocolate	• Place plain and milk chocolate, butter, and golden syrup in the saucepan.
150g	Milk chocolate	• Keeping a low heat, gently melt the chocolate, butter, and syrup but do not boil.
100g	Unsalted butter	• Allow to cool.
140g	Golden syrup	

Group B

250g	Digestive biscuits	• Place the digestive biscuits in a bowl and break the biscuits into small pieces but not to a crumb.
100g	Pink and white mini marshmallows	• Add the melted ingredients from Group A into the biscuits and mix together. • Now add the marshmallows and mix them all together until all covered with the chocolate. • Line the baking tray with parchment paper. • Pour the mixture into the tray and level the mixture evenly across the tray. • Leave in the fridge until set. • The rocky road can be cut into fingers or squares.

• This mix is not baked but as a firm favourite had to be part of the book.

• This recipe I have used for three wedding cakes now. I skim the rocky road with ganache to create sharp edges.

Apricot Jane's Hints and Tips

- It cuts well without being too crumbly.

- Use a good couverture chocolate; it is worth it for the flavour.

Dome Carrot Cake

This deliciously moist carrot cake has everyone coming back for more. We made this in a slab and cut it into squares for our college shop. It sold out every day.

Equipment:	Scales, measuring spoons, bowls, mixer, whisk attachment, spatula, grater, 17cm (6") half sphere mould (or 2 x 18cm (7") round tins), cooling wire, palette knife, serrated knife, turntable.
Oven:	Pre-heat to 180°C, 170°C fan (350°F); Gas 4.

Group A

90g (2)	Egg	• Mix the egg and sugar together to start dissolving the sugar.
180g	Dark brown sugar	• Whisk together until a foam is reached on a medium speed. The mix will be thick and will get lighter in colour during whisking.

Group B

75g	Vegetable oil	• Add to Group A in a steady stream on low speed.

Group C

110g	Strong flour	• Sieve together.
1tsp	Cinnamon	• Add to Group A and Group B.
¼ tsp	Bicarbonate of soda	• Gently mix on low speed until the batter is smooth and there are no signs of flour.
½tsp	Baking powder	

Group D

200g	Grated carrot	• Fold in the carrot, walnuts, and dates with a spatula until all ingredients are blended together. Be careful not to knock the air out.
30g	Chopped walnuts	• Grease and flour the half sphere mould (or round tins).
30g	Chopped dried dates	• Deposit the batter into the half sphere mould (or round tins, with 335g of batter mix per tin for a round cake).
		• Bake the sphere for 45 minutes (round cakes 30-35 minutes).
		• When baked, remove from the tins and place on the cooling wire.

Filling and Topping		Group E
100g	Full fat cream cheese	• Beat the butter, vanilla, and icing sugar together until light and creamy.
100g	Softened butter	• Soften the cream cheese and add to the butter and icing; don't over-mix.
100g	Icing sugar	• Colour 5g of the marzipan green and the remainder of the marzipan orange.
1 tsp	Vanilla	• Divide the paste into 6 even pieces – about 2.5g each.
20g	Marzipan	• Make six carrots from the orange marzipan; mark a line across them; place a little
Colours	Green /orange	green leaf on top to complete.

Assembly

- Cut the dome into 3 layers.
- Spread a little of the cream filling in each layer and assemble the dome.
- Using a palette knife, skim the dome with cream filling and chill in the fridge.
- Colour about 100g of the cream filling orange.
- Remove the dome from the fridge and cover with the vanilla cream filling; then touch up with random orange around the dome. This will give a toned colour finish.
- Place on the turntable, and with the palette knife, hold on a 45° angle and evenly rotate the table, slowly moving the palette knife evenly down as you create an even ridge.
- Place a bulb on the top of the dome and arrange the carrots around the top.

Apricot Jane's
Hints and Tips

- Dissolving the sugar in the first stage helps to get a smooth texture and more volume.

- This method also helps give a spongy texture.

- The oil helps to give moisture and softness to the cake crumb.

- Strong flour helps to give structure to the cake. Since there are many carrots, the cake batter becomes more fluid.

- Creaming the softened butter first really helps to stabilise the cream cheese and helps to avoid splitting of the cream.

- Take the cream cheese out of the fridge and let it come to an ambient temperature. If it is too cold, it will split the mix.

- If you are using 18cm (7") cake tins, cut each cake into two and fill each layer with the cream filling. Assemble and cover the whole cake with the cream filling.

Sticky Spiced Apple and Apricot Buns

A lovely spiced sticky bun finger-licking good.

Equipment:	Scales, measuring spoons, bowl, scraper, baking tray 30 x 20cm (12 x 8"), saucepan, piping bag, pastry brush, cling film or damp cloth.
Oven:	Pre-heat to 200°C, 190°C fan (400°F); Gas 5.
Dough temperature:	26°C (78°F).
Yield:	6 buns.

Group A

225g	Strong flour	• Rub the butter into the flour
25g	Butter	

Group B

10g	Milk powder	• Add the milk powder, sugar, salt, cinnamon, and yeast; mix through the flour and butter crumble.
15g	Caster Sugar	
3g (¾ tsp)	Salt	• Make a well and add warm water.
2g (½ tsp)	Cinnamon	• Mix together to form a dough.
4g (½ tbsp)	Dried yeast	• Knead the dough to develop; this will take about 8 minutes and it should then be smooth and elastic.
125ml	Warm water	
		• Cover with cling film or a damp cloth. Prove for 1 hour, then knock back the dough and leave for a further 15 minutes.

Group C

30g	Butter	• Cream the butter, cinnamon, and sugar together until light and creamy.
40g	Soft light brown sugar	• Peel and cut the apple into small cubes.
2g (½ tsp)	Cinnamon	• Add the apricots and apple to the creamed mixture.
40g	Chopped apricots	
1	Braeburn apple	
½tsp	Baking powder	

Process

- After the proof, weigh the dough into approximately 65g pieces to make 6 buns.
- Mould into round balls and re-cover to rest for 5 minutes.
- Re-mould the buns and place them on a baking tray, allowing space for them to grow.
- Prove the dough buns for about 20 minutes.

- Make an indent in the middle of each proved dough bun. Egg wash the buns and deposit a dessert spoonful of the apple and apricot filling from Group C into the centre of each bun.
- Prove again for about 5 minutes.
- Bake for 15-20 minutes.

Group D

50g	Apricot jam
½	Juice of lemon
70g	Icing sugar

- Boil the apricot jam and brush gently over the buns when they come out of the oven.
- Mix the icing sugar and lemon juice together. Depending on the amount of juice the lemon gives you, you may need a little extra icing sugar – consistency should just be able to hold its shape.
- Cool the buns before spiral piping the icing over the buns.

Apricot Jane's
Hints and Tips

- Dough temperature is important to achieve the best results. The yeast works best at 26°C. This is explained fully in the Section on Bread on page 15.

- If the Bun is too warm when piping on the lemon icing, it will dissolve into the Bun, and the icing effect will be lost.

- You can divide any spare dough around the buns, so there is no waste.

- Make the indent big enough to hold the filling.

  The apricot glaze will keep the fruit looking lush and fresh.

  The buns are best eaten on the day of Baking!

Sausage, Bacon, and Mushroom Puff Pie

As the weather changes, who doesn't love a sausage pie? So comforting. A great family favourite.

Equipment:	Scales, measuring spoons, rolling pin, bowls, frying pan, spatula, baking tray 30 x 20cm (12 x 8"), pastry brush.
Oven:	Pre-heat to 200°C, 190°C fan (400°F); Gas 6.

Group A

15g (1 tbsp)	Oil	• Place the oil in the frying pan and heat gently.
1	Chopped onion	• Add the chopped onions and cook without colour; then remove and place in a bowl.
4	Chopped rashers of bacon	• Add the bacon to the frying pan, and cook gently without colour, not dark or crispy.
100g	Sliced mushroom	• Add the sliced mushrooms and lightly cook with the bacon.
		• Place the bacon and mushrooms in the bowl with the onion.

Filling — Group B

500g	Sausage meat	• Place all Group B ingredients in a bowl and mix together thoroughly.
15g (1 tbsp)	Grain mustard	• Add the onions, bacon, and mushrooms to the Group B ingredients and blend together using a spatula.
60g	Dried breadcrumbs	• Cover the mix with cling film and place it in the fridge until required.
¼ tsp	Salt	
¼ tsp	Pepper	
25g	Creme fraiche	

Puff pastry — Group C

340g	Strong flour	• Rub the butter into the flour.
40g	Butter	• Add water to make a dough, using the dough hook attachment.
1g	Salt	• Mix to develop for 8 minutes at No 1 (slowest) speed.
200g	Water	• Rest the dough for 10 minutes.

Group D

225g	Butter	• Follow the English method for making puff pastry as described in Section on Puff Pastry on page 37.
		• Give the pastry 6 half turns.
		• Rest the pastry before processing.

Process

- Roll out half the pastry to 3mm thick and 18 x 10cm (7 x 4").
- Place the filling in the centre of the pastry, leaving a 3cm (1") edge all the way around.
- Using a pastry brush, egg wash the edge all the way around.
- Roll out the remaining pastry a little larger than the base to allow for the height when covering the sausage meat mix.
- Cover over the sausage meat with the above rolled-out pastry, pressing down the pastry onto the egg wash so that it attaches.
- Trim the edges of the pastry, then crimp around the edge of the pastry to seal in the filling.
- Using the pastry brush, gently brush egg wash over the top of the pastry.
- Make a hole in the top to let out the steam.
- The top can be decorated with some of the left-over pastry cut into leaves and arranged on top.
- Rest for 20 minutes before baking.
- Bake for 40 minutes until golden and crisp.

Apricot Jane's
Hints and Tips

- Detailed notes on the puff pastry methods can be found in the Section on Puff Pastry on page 37.

- If you can't get sausage meat, just skin the sausage and remove the meat.

- You can develop the flavours you like by the type of sausage you buy.

- The Breadcrumbs help to absorb the fat from the sausage.

- A hole in the top of the pastry allows the steam to escape and helps to keep the lid on.

Spiced Plum Choux

Plums are a forgotten fruit in the bakery, so I thought, as it is autumn, I would spice them up and include them in a choux bun which makes a lovely change.

Equipment:	Scales, measuring spoons, saucepan, bowls, spatula, baking tray 30 x 20 cm (12 x 8") 3.5cm cutter, 4cm silicone pebble mould, piping bags, plain 1cm tube, small star tube, sieve.
Oven:	Pre-heat to 190°C, 180°C fan (375°F); Gas 5.

Craquelin — Group A

20g	Butter	• Cream the butter and sugar together.
25g	Demerara sugar	• Add the flour and mix to a paste; leave to rest in the fridge for 15 minutes.
25g	Plain flour	• Roll out the paste to 3mm thick and cut 3.5mm circles.
		• Place the circles on a sheet of parchment paper and freeze until required.

Spiced Plum Mousse — Group B

250g	Red plums	• Slice the plums; remove the stones.
30g	Caster sugar	• Place the plums, sugar, wine, cinnamon, star anise, cardamom pods, zest, and juice
40ml	Red wine	of the orange into a saucepan and cook gently until the plums are cooked, holding
1 zest and juice	Orange	their shape.
1	Cinnamon stick	
1	Star anise	
6	Cardamom pods	
5g (2 leaves)	Gelatine	
80ml	Double cream	

To make the mousse:
- Place the gelatine in cold water to soften.
- Take 200g of the hot plum mix; place it in a bowl, and add the softened gelatine.
- Allow the gelatine to melt in the plum mix; allow to cool.
- Whisk the double cream to a soft peak and fold it into the cooled plum mixture.
- Deposit the mousse into a 4cm silicone pebble mould.
- Place in the freezer until required.

Choux — Group C

125ml	Water
50g	Salted butter
¼tsp	Sugar
65g	Plain flour
100g (2)	Egg

- Place the water and butter with the sugar into the saucepan.
- Bring to a boil; remove from the heat.
- Add the flour and beat into the boiled water and butter until it leaves the side of the pan.
- Return to the heat and cook out the mix to gelatinise the starch.
- Transfer the mix to a bowl and allow it to cool.
- Add the egg gradually to the paste and beat well until a dropping consistency is obtained. (This is done by scooping up some paste with the spatula and allowing it to drop; the paste will drop, leaving a V shape (The paste should not flow)
- Place into a piping bag with a plain 1cm tube.
- Pipe even bulbs 3cm in diameter.
- Then take out the craquelin discs and place on top of the bulbs.
- Bake for 25 minutes, then drop the temperature to 170°C, 160°C fan (355°F), Gas 4, for 5 minutes to dry out.

Assembly — Group D

220ml	Double cream
1	Plum
20g	Icing sugar

- Whisk the cream to a piping consistency.
- Then place it in a piping bag with a star tube.
- Slice the plums to be used as garnish.

- Cut the choux bun in half sideways.
- Place the remaining plums on the base of the choux bun.
- Pipe a rosette of cream on top.
- Then place the plum mousse on top of the cream.
- Pipe a rosette of cream on top and place the choux lid on top and a slice of plum on the side.
- Dust lightly with icing sugar.

- There is a lot of water in the choux recipe, so the choux will need to be baked at a high temperature, so the water turns to steam and expands the choux making the inside hollow.

Apricot Jane's
Hints and Tips

- Always ensure that the choux has been cooked out well; when the starch gelatinises, it can absorb the egg. The egg proteins and gelatinised starch help create a wall.

- The choux will need to be set and dried out, so removing the choux too early from the oven leads to collapse.

- It is possible to adapt the mousse filling to a flavours of your choice, e.g., apple, rhubarb, apricot, and chocolate.

- The craquelin top gives an interesting texture. If you want, you can replace some of the flour with ground nuts. Also, it could be coloured to represent the internal flavours.

Coffee and Walnut Drip Cake

Try this lovely moist textured cake with a cup of coffee.

Equipment:	Scales, measuring spoons, mixer with beater and whisk attachments, bowls, saucepan, hand whisk, 3 x 18cm (6") sponge tins, cooling wire, 2 x piping bags, small star tube for rosettes.
Oven:	Pre-heat to 180°C, 170°C fan (350°F); Gas 4.

Coffee cake — Group A

200g	Butter	• Using the mixer with the paddle attachment, cream the butter and sugar together until light and creamy.
50g	Shortening (e.g., Trex)	• Gradually add the eggs, beating well between each addition.
175g	Light brown sugar	
175g (3)	Eggs	

Group B

135g	Plain flour	• Grease and flour the sides of the tins and place a parchment disc on the base of each one.
50g	Ground almonds	
5g (1 tsp)	Baking powder	• Dissolve the coffee granules in the boiled water.
15g (1 tbsp)	Instant coffee granules	• Add the coffee to the batter.
		• Fold in the flour and walnuts into the batter.
10ml (1 tsp)	Boiling water	• Deposit the cake mix in 230g into the prepared tins.
75g	Chopped walnuts	• Place in the oven and bake for 25 minutes at 180°C, 170°C fan.
		• When baked, cool for five minutes in the tin, then deposit onto a cooling wire.

Swiss Buttercream — Group C

100g (2)	Egg white	• Dissolve the coffee granules in the boiling water.
200g	Caster sugar	• Place the egg white and sugar in a bowl and place over a saucepan of water.
250g	Unsalted softened butter	• Heat the whites and sugar gently over the hot water and whisk until the sugar granules are dissolved.
10 (1 heaped tbsp)	Instant coffee granules	• Remove from the heat; transfer to mixing bowl and whisk attachment.
15ml (1 tbsp)	Boiled water	• Whisk until a foam is created and cold.
75g	Chopped walnuts	• Gradually add the butter into the foam until completely mixed to form a lovely smooth buttercream.
		• Add the coffee into the buttercream.

Ganache for drip	Group D

100g	Chocolate	• Place the cream into the saucepan and bring to a boil.
50ml	Double cream	• Pour over the chocolate; leave for a few minutes to let the chocolate melt.
10g	Butter	• Mix together until smooth. When cooled, add the butter to the ganache.
8	Walnut halves	• Place in a piping bag.

Assembly

- Cut each sponge in two.
- Spread a thin layer of the coffee buttercream onto each layer.
- When all the layers are assembled, coat the side and top of the cake with a thin layer of the buttercream.
- Set in the fridge for about 10 minutes.
- Remove from the fridge and apply another thin coat of buttercream around the side. The top can be textured to give interest. Set again in the fridge for about 10 minutes.
- Remove from the fridge. With the piping bag of soft ganache, drip around the top of the cake, allowing the chocolate to flow; unevenly is fine.
- With the remaining buttercream, pipe six or eight rosettes and then place a walnut half on each rosette.

• The chocolate ganache could be poured on the cake to cover the top if so desired, then allow the drips to flow.

• The sides of the cake could be textured or even left naked.

Apricot Jane's

Hints and Tips

Sticky Toffee Pudding

There is nothing better than on a cold day to comfort yourself with this luxurious sticky toffee pudding flowing with toffee sauce and delicious with ice cream.

Equipment:	Scales, measuring spoons, saucepan, spatula, bowls, either one 25 x 20 x 4cm deep (10 x 8 x 1.5″ deep) dish or 6 pudding moulds for individual puddings.
Oven:	Pre-heat to 180°C, 170°C fan (350°F); Gas 4.
Yield:	This recipe makes one large or 6 individual puddings.

Group A

175g	Stoned chopped dried dates	• Bring the water to a boil.
200ml	Boiling water	• Add the chopped dates.
5g (1 tsp)	Bicarbonate of soda	• Add the bicarbonate of soda and leave to cool.

Group B

75g	Unsalted butter	• Cream the butter and sugar until light and creamy.
150g	Dark soft brown sugar	• Add the eggs in stages to form a smooth batter.
120g (2)	Egg	

Group C

175g	Plain flour	• Add the dry ingredients into the Group B batter.
5g (1 tsp)	Baking powder	• Blend together.
80g	Chopped pecan nuts	• Add the dates and water to the batter – it will become thinner; this is fine.

Deposit

- Grease and flour the dish or the 6 pudding moulds.
- Place all the batter into the prepared dish, or 120g per individual pudding mould.
- Bake for 30 minutes (for the dish) or 25 minutes (for the moulds).

Toffee sauce		Group D
100g	Unsalted butter	• Melt the butter and sugar together in a saucepan and boil for 2 minutes.
150g	Soft brown sugar	• Remove from the heat and add the cream.
150ml	Double cream	• Blend together.
100g	Fudge pieces	

Serving

- For the single pudding in a dish:
  When it comes out of the oven, use the end of a wooden spoon to make holes. Fill each cavity with the toffee sauce ready for serving.

- For the individual puddings:
  Remove from the mould and place on a plate. Make a hole in the centre with the end of the wooden spoon. Fill the cavity with the sauce and let it run over. Sprinkle the fudge pieces on the top and serve with crème fraiche or ice cream.

Apricot Jane's
Hints and Tips

- Soaking the dates:

  a) helps to increase volume and

  b) softens the skins and helps break them down so that they are easily dispersed through the mix and don't sink.

- Double cream is best, as it has a higher fat content, and enriches the toffee sauce.

WINTER

On cold dark nights,
The lights do twinkle,
Time for mulled wine,
and comfort food, with friends

A collection of festive recipes to
make, bake, and enjoy the season
with family and friends.

Sticky Clementine Ginger Cake

A sticky ginger cake is so delicious any time of the year, so I gave this one a festive feel with clementines and a decorative finish.

| Equipment: | Scales, measuring spoons, small saucepan, spatula, whisk, pastry brush, mixing bowl 22cm (9"), savarin mould 18cm (7") diameter. |
| **Oven:** | Pre-heat to 190°C, 180°C fan (375°F); Gas 5. |

Group A

65g	Butter	• Place butter, dark brown sugar, and treacle into a saucepan.
90g	Dark brown sugar	• Melt the butter, dissolve the sugar, bring to a boil and remove from the heat.
75g	Treacle	

Group B

120g	Yoghurt or Buttermilk	• Blend together the yoghurt, egg, zest, and juice.
50g (1)	Egg	• Add the cooled Group A ingredients and blend together with a whisk.
Zest and juice of 1	Clementine	

Group C

90g	Plain flour	• Sieve together all dry ingredients into a bowl.
30g	Wholemeal flour	• Then add to the combined liquids of Groups A and B and whisk together to form a smooth batter.
5g (1 tsp)	Ground ginger	• Deposit into the prepared tin (if it is non-stick, spray with fat, otherwise, grease and flour).
2g (½ tsp)	Cinnamon	• Bake for 25 minutes.
4g (¾ tsp)	Bicarbonate soda	• When baked, the cake should spring back when touched in the centre.
2g (½ tsp)	Baking powder	• Remove from the tin and cool on a wire rack.
2g (½ tsp)	Nutmeg	

Topping		Group D
Juice of 1	Clementine	• Boil the apricot jam with a little water and brush over the ginger cake.
¼tsp	Orange extract	• Blend the clementine juice and orange extract together.
125g approx	Sieved icing sugar	• Add the icing sugar enough so that it can be drizzled.
30g	Apricot jam	• Place the icing into a piping bag and drizzle over the cake; allow the drips to flow unevenly.

Decorative finish		Group E
6 pieces of	Crystalised ginger	• Decorate by arranging the ginger, cherries, and pistachio in six segments on the top.
3	Glacé cherries cut into six pieces	• Scatter the gold pearls at random.
10g	Chopped pistachio (six pieces)	• Lightly coat with gold glitter spray to give a festive sheen.
20	Gold pearls	
	Gold glitter spray	

Apricot Jane's Hints and Tips

• You can change the yoghurt for Buttermilk or even quark, which helps to give a better flavour.

• Treacle helps to give colour and provides moisture and softness in the cake crumb. It also helps to give stickiness to the cake.

• Using bicarbonate of soda helps with aeration and crumb colour and works well with the dark brown sugar and treacle.

• A great alternative for Christmas.

Panettone

Panettone is a light Italian enriched sweet bread. Serve with coffee to celebrate the season.

Equipment: Scales, measuring spoons, bowl, 20cm (8") round tin, thermometer, oiled cling film.

Oven: Pre-heat to 180°C, 170°C fan (375°F); Gas 5.

Dough temperature: 26°C (78°F). See Hints and Tips.

Preparation time: This recipe involves leaving the fruit overnight.

Fruit — Group A

100g	Raisins	• Place all these ingredients in a bowl and allow the flavour to be absorbed into the fruit; leave overnight if possible for the best results.
30g	Cranberries	
45g	Chopped dried apricot	
40g	Mixed peel	
40g	Chopped cherries	
1tsp	Vanilla extract	
1 ½ tbsp	Rum	
1 zest	Lemon	
1 zest	Orange	

Sugar batter — Group B

250g	Salted butter	• Cream the butter and sugar together until light and creamy.
100g	Caster sugar	• Gradually add the eggs and milk.
4	Eggs	
2 tbsp	Milk	

Dough — Group C

7g (1 sachet)	Dried yeast	• Blend the flour and yeast together.
300g	Strong flour	• Add the flour and yeast to the sugar batter mix (Group B) to make the dough.
		• Knead this to develop into a smooth dough.
		• Place in a bowl, cover with oiled cling film, and leave in a warm place for one and half hours.

Process

- Add the fruit from Group A to the dough and work it through.
- Leave to recover for a further 30 minutes.
- Line the tin with parchment to at least 6cm (2") above the top of the tin.
- Hand mould the dough into a ball and place it in the prepared tin.
- Cover over and leave to prove in a warm place until double the size. This takes about 30 minutes.
- Gently egg wash the top of the dough.
- Bake for 25 minutes; tap the base – it should sound hollow when ready.
- Remove from the oven; cool, and dust with icing sugar.

Apricot Jane's

Hints and Tips

- Panettone is classified as an enriched dough. It is cake-like in texture.

- Dough temperature is important to achieve the best results. The yeast works best at 26°C. This is explained fully in the Section on Bread on page 15.

- Any leftover is great in a Bread and Butter pudding.

Chocolate Mint Mousse Roulade

I have made this roulade in green, so when it is cut, you get a lovely surprise, and the mint ganache complements it beautifully.

Equipment:	Scales, measuring spoon, mixer with a whisk attachment, bowl, saucepan, spatula, sieve, baking tray 30 x 20cm (12 x 8"), greaseproof paper, palette knife, cooling wire, piping bag, 1cm plain piping tube.
Oven:	Pre-heat to 200°C, 190°C fan (400°F); Gas 6.

Roulade		Group A
150g (3)	Large eggs	• Whisk the eggs and caster sugar and spring green colour together. The foam should be at the ribbon stage, i.e., leaves a trace and holds its shape.
100g	Caster sugar	• Sieve the plain flour onto the foam and fold in carefully until the flour has been evenly distributed. Do not overhandle as the air will be knocked out.
75g	Plain flour	• Line the baking tray with greaseproof paper.
¼ tsp	Spring green colour	• Pour the mixture onto the prepared baking tray and level the sponge using a palette knife.
		• Bake for 12 to 15 minutes.
		• Place some parchment paper on the table; dust it liberally with caster sugar then tip the roulade onto the parchment. Leave the tin on top of the roulade until cold.

Mint mousse		Group B
60g	Milk	• Bring the milk to a boil in a saucepan; remove from the heat.
100g	Dark chocolate couverture	• Pour the milk over the chocolate and leave for a few minutes to melt the chocolate.
1 tsp	Peppermint extract	• Add the peppermint extract and whisk together until it is smooth; allow to cool.
150ml	Double cream	• Whisk the cream until it has soft peaks.
		• Gently fold the cream into the cooled chocolate mix.

Process

- Remove the tray from the roulade.
- Carefully remove the greaseproof paper from the roulade.
- Spread the mint mousse evenly on top of the roulade sponge.
- Then grasp the long side of the sponge and roll it towards yourself, keeping the shape firm and bold; then trim the edges (The second picture in the Apricot and Mixed Fruit Stollen recipe on page 171 shows how this rolling is done)
- Place the roulade onto a cooling wire.

Coating and topping   Group C

50ml	Whipping cream	
7g (1 tsp)	Glucose	
60g	Dark chocolate couverture	
40g	Milk chocolate couverture	
1 tsp	Peppermint extract	
10g	Softened butter	
2	After Eight mints	
2	Mint matchsticks	
10g	Hundreds and Thousands	

- Boil the cream and glucose together.
- Pour the mix over the chocolate and leave for a few minutes. Until the chocolate begins to melt.
- Mix the chocolate and cream together to emulsify; the chocolate should then be smooth and lump free.
- Cool before adding the softened butter to the ganache (the chocolate/cream mix).
- Place the roulade on a cooling wire.
- Using a palette knife, thinly skim the ganache over the Swiss roll (This will seal the crumb, ready for the main coat).
- Allow the ganache to set.

Finishing process

- The ganache needs to be able to flow. If it has cooled down too much, gently warm the ganache.
- Starting at one end of the roll, pour the ganache evenly over the roll to completely cover it. Tap the wire to encourage the flow.
- Gather up the ganache that has flowed off.
- Beat the remaining ganache until it thickens; then place it in a piping bag with a plain 1cm tube.
- Evenly pipe 8 bulbs along the top middle of the roulade.
- Cut each After Eight mint into 4 triangles; dip their edges into the Hundreds and Thousands.
- Place on top of the ganache bulb.
- Cut each of the mint matchsticks into 4 and place them behind the mint Christmas tree to complete.

Apricot Jane's Hints and Tips

- Leaving the roulade to cool on the parchment with the tray left on top traps the moisture in the sponge and keeps it soft and pliable when required to roll.

- Over whipping the cream makes the mousse bitty in texture and not smooth.

- Lightly skimming the roll with the ganache before the main coating ensures that the ganache will attach well and give a smoother finish.

- Ganache can be used at various stages, and as it cools, the ganache will thicken, thus enabling you to pipe bulbs.

Gingerbread Men

These little guys are fun to make and can be wrapped and given as gifts at Christmas.

Equipment: Scales, measuring spoons, deep saucepan, spatula, rolling pin, baking tray 30 x 20cm (12 x 8") lined with parchment, sieve, small knife, template for large gingerbread man 28 x 20cm (11 x 8") hand mixer with a whisk attachment, bowl.

Oven: Pre-heat to 190°C, 180°C fan (375°F); Gas 5.

Yield: 7 large gingerbread men.

Gingerbread		Group A
240g	Golden syrup	• Place syrup, butter, and soft brown sugar in a deep saucepan.
150g	Butter	• Melt the butter and dissolve the sugar.
150g	Soft brown sugar	• Bring to a boil.
		• Remove from the heat.

Foam mixture		Group B
30g	Bicarbonate of soda	• Mix the water and bicarbonate of soda together in a bowl.
60g	Cold water	• Add to the hot syrup mixture. The mix will foam up; this is ok.
160g	Egg	

		Group C
800g	Plain flour	• Sieve the flour and ginger together into a bowl.
30g	Ginger powder	• Make a well.
		• Add the egg and foam mixture to the well.
		• With a spatula, incorporate the flour to form a paste.
		• Keep the dough wrapped and warm.

Process

- Roll out enough paste to fit the template to 6mm thick.
- Place the paste onto the prepared baking tray.
- Using the template and a small sharp knife, cut around the template.
- Gently soften the edges by using your finger to get rid of any rough edges.

- Bake for 20 minutes until golden.
- Remove from the oven and allow to cool on the baking tray.

Do not remove them from the tray until they are cold to ensure the paste has set. There is then less chance of the gingerbread breaking.

Foam mixture		Group D
80g	Egg whites	• Sterilise the bowl and hand mixer in boiling water to ensure they are grease free.
500g	Icing sugar	• Mix the egg white and icing together in the bowl to form a soft peak; this will take about ten minutes. This is royal icing.
50g	Hundreds and Thousands	• Keep the mix covered in a damp cloth to ensure no skin forms.
20g	Ready to roll fondant Black colouring	• Roll out the ready-to-roll paste in 2 x 2cm diameter discs for each gingerbread man.

- Spread each disc with the royal icing and dip it in the Hundreds and Thousands.
- Attach the buttons on each gingerbread man's tummy with a spot of royal icing.
- Colour some royal icing black to pipe on the eyes.
- Pipe a mouth in white icing and a little white across each leg and arm.
- Roll out a strip of paste to make a scarf. This can be dipped in the Hundreds and Thousands and attached with icing around the neck.

Apricot Jane's Hints and Tips

- It is important to make sure the equipment used for beating the egg white and icing sugar is completely clean and sterilised because any grease will cause the mix to lack volume and drop.

- Adding the bicarbonate of soda to the warm mix will create air bubbles quickly, and the mix will foam up. When baked, this gives a soft texture but firm enough to hold its shape.

- The bicarbonate of soda helps with the colour of the paste when it is baked.

- There is enough mixture here to make a gingerbread house if you would prefer.

- There is a template for the gingerbread man at the back of the book – see the Section on Templates on page 195.

Roasted Red Pepper Pesto Star

When I made this for a Boxing Day get-together, it went down a storm, served warm with all the wonderful ham, turkey, cheese, and chutneys.

Equipment: Scales, measuring spoons, bowl, dough scraper, baking tray 30 x 20 cm (12 x 8"), 5.5cm round cutter, 2.5cm round cutter, sharp knife, pastry brush, rolling pin, silicon paper, cling film or damp cloth.

Oven: Pre-heat to 200°C, 190°C fan (400°F); Gas 6.

Dough temperature: 26°C (78°F). See Hints and Tips.

Dough stage 1		Group A
325g	Strong flour	• Rub the butter into the flour.
35g	Garlic butter	

Dough stage 2		Group B
3g (¾ tsp)	Sugar	• Add the salt, sugar, and dried yeast to the Group A mix.
10g (½ tbsp)	Salt	• Make a well and add the egg, milk, and water – mix to form a dough.
7g (1 sachet)	Dried yeast	• Knead for 8-10 minutes to develop the dough until smooth and elastic.
1	Egg	• Cover with cling film or a damp cloth, prove for one hour in a warm place, and then knock back the dough.
100ml	Warm water	• Return to prove for a further 15 minutes.
40ml	Warm milk	• Divide the dough into 4 x 145g pieces and mould each into a round shape.
		• Rest the dough for five minutes.
		• Roll out each piece of dough into 18cm discs, resting each between rolling as the dough will spring back.

		Group C
50g	Roasted red pepper pesto	• See Assembly below.
20g	Sesame seeds	

Assembly

- Place the first disc on a sheet of silicone paper, then spread the pesto from the centre out to the edge of the disc.
- Lay the next disc on top and spread pesto on that one. Repeat until the last disc is placed on top, making a stack of four.

Sectioning

- Mark the centre of the dough with the 5.5cm cutter but don't cut right through.
- With the sharp knife, cut through the dough from the edge of the circle, dividing the circle into 4.
- Then cut each section into 4 equal smaller segments.
- This will make 16 segments.
- As in the picture, take two adjacent segments and give the one on the left hand one twist to the left and the one on the right hand one twist to the right; then join the two edges together, so the top of the dough sits side by side.

Finishing and baking

- As in the picture, continue this until all pieces have been twisted – the internal lines will be visible, making a pattern.
- Egg wash the centre circle; then place the 2.5cm cutter on top. Fill the cavity with sesame seeds; tap down gently, then carefully remove the cutter.
- Gently egg wash the dough.
- Prove the dough for about 30 minutes in a warm place.
- Bake for 25 minutes.

- Dough temperature is important to achieve the best results. The yeast works best at 26°C. This is explained fully in the Section on Bread on page 15.

- For the filling, you could also use green pesto sauce or cream cheese with chives.

- Don't overfill because it makes it difficult to twist.

- This is a great tear and share bread and goes well with a hearty soup.

Apricot and Mixed Fruit Stollen

This is a delicious fruited bread with marzipan with a hint of rum, making a special Christmas treat.

Equipment: Scales, measuring spoons, bowl, rolling pin, sharp knife, pastry brush, baking tray 30 x 20cm (12 x 8"), sieve, small saucepan, thermometer, cling film or damp cloth.

Oven: Pre-heat to 190°C, 180°C fan (400°F); Gas 6.

Dough temperature: 26°C (78°F)

Dough		Group A
360g	Strong flour	• Rub the butter into the flour.
35g	Butter	

		Group B
2g (¾ tsp)	Mixed spice	• Blend together the dried ingredients.
25g	Caster sugar	• Make a well in the centre.
7g (1 sachet)	Dried Yeast	
2g (½ tsp)	Salt	

		Group C
1	Egg	• Add the egg and milk into the well and bring together to form a dough.
180ml	Warm milk	• Knead to develop the dough for about 10 minutes.
		• Place the dough into a bowl, cover with cling film or a damp cloth, and leave in a warm place to prove for 1 hour.

		Group D
60g	Chopped apricots	• Place the chopped apricot, sultanas, and cherries in a bowl.
40g	Sultanas	• Add the zest, orange juice, and rum and leave for 30 minutes to allow the fruits to absorb the flavours.
4	Chopped cherries	
5ml	Rum	• After 1 hour of proof, add half the fruit to the dough and leave to prove for a further 20 minutes.
½	Orange juice	

Group E

125g	Grated marzipan	• Roll out the dough to 30 x 20cm (12 x 8") so the top of the dough is the same as the width of the baking tray.
25g	Flaked almonds	
1	Orange zest and juice	• Sprinkle the zest of orange over the surface of the dough.
1	Egg wash	• Sprinkle the remainder of the fruit mix over the dough.

Process

- Evenly grate the marzipan over the fruit.
- Leave 3cm (1") of dough at the front edge without fillings, and egg wash that strip. This will help the dough to stick.

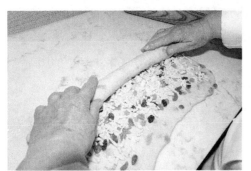

- Roll from the top to the base, gently pulling to create a firm roll of dough.
- Ensure the dough edge is sealed.
- Gently extend the length on the roll to about 40cm (15").

- With the sharp knife, cut longways straight down the centre of the roll. Slightly open to reveal the fruits.

- Twist the two pieces together like a two-strand plait.

- From one end in the centre, wrap the remainder of the two-strand plait around and secure the end underneath, creating a round shape.

- Lightly egg wash and sprinkle with the flaked almonds.
- Cover over with cling film and leave to prove until double the size.
- Bake for 25 minutes until lightly golden.

Group F		

20g	Melted butter	• When the stollen is removed from the oven, gently brush over with the melted butter and rum.
20ml	Rum	• Dust over with the icing sugar.
50g	Icing sugar	• Repeat with the butter and rum and give a good final dusting of icing to finish.

Apricot Jane's
Hints and Tips

• Dough temperature is important to achieve the best results. The yeast works best at 26°C. This is explained fully in the Section on Bread on page 15.

• Traditionally the marzipan is rolled into a sausage shape and placed in the dough, so when cut, the marzipan is visible.

- I have experimented with grating the marzipan across the rolled-out dough and found that it keeps the dough lovely and moist and distributes the flavour through the whole dough.

- This stollen could also be done as a slab tray 30 x 20cm – divide the dough in half, roll out, and line the tray, then add the zest, fruit, and grated marzipan. Roll out the remaining dough and place it on top of the fruits. Prove, bake, and finish as above.

Rich Fruit Genoa Cake

A lovely fruity nutty-topped rich fruit cake. Great if you don't have time to marzipan and ice the cake. This can be eaten any time of the year for all you fruit cake lovers.

Equipment: Scales, measuring spoons, chopping board, knife, bowl, mixer with a beater attachment, scraper, 20cm round cake tin., parchment paper, thin needle.

Oven: Pre-heat to 140°C, 130°C fan (275°F); Gas 1.

Dough temperature: This recipe involves preparing the fruit a day in advance.

Fruit		Group A
275g	Currants	• Chop the apricots and cut the cherries in half.
175g	Sultanas	• Place all the currants, sultanas, raisins, apricots, peel, and cherries in a bowl.
75g	Raisins	• Add the zest and juice of lemon and the brandy (optional).
75g	Dried apricots	• For best results, prepare this the day before.
75g	Chopped peel	
75g	Glacé cherries	
1 zest & juice	Lemon	
20ml	Brandy	

Batter		Group B
175g	Butter	• Using the mixer and beater attachment, cream together the butter, soft brown sugar, and treacle until light and creamy.
175g	Soft dark brown sugar	
1 tbsp	Black treacle	• Add the eggs in four stages, beating well and scraping around the bowl between each addition.
200g (4)	Eggs	

		Group C
200g	Plain flour	• Add all the dry ingredients to the creamed batter from Group B.
50g	Ground Almonds	• Mix until all the dry ingredients have been evenly distributed.
2 tsp	Mixed spice	• Gently add all Group A fruits into the batter and mix in using a spatula, so the fruits don't get crushed.
		• Line the cake tin with parchment paper on the sides and base.
		• Deposit into the tin; press down and smooth the top.

Group D

100g	Glacé cherries
100g	Whole Brazil nuts
150g	Pecan nuts

- Arrange the pecan nuts around the top edge of the cake.
- Then in front of the pecan nuts, place a row of glacé cherries.
- In front of the cherries, place a row of Brazil nuts.
- Place a glacé cherry in the centre and then fill the gap with small pecan nuts.
- The whole top will be covered in fruit and nuts.
- Bake on the middle shelf for about 2½ hours.
- To check that the cake is baked, push a thin needle in the centre of the cake – it should come out clean.
- When baked, leave to cool in the tin.

• Leaving the fruit in Group A to mature overnight develops the flavours, and the fruit will plump up.

• The nuts and fruit on top can be changed if so desired.

• When it comes out of the oven, I always place a solid cover over the cake. This traps the moisture – it gives the cake a soft crust and keeps the cake moist.

• This cake will mature with age, so it can be made in advance and kept in an air-tight container for up to six months (if you can wait that long).

• This recipe could also be used for a Christmas cake, in which case, leave the fruit and nuts off the top so that you can cover it with marzipan and icing.

Mocha and Baileys Mousse Tartlet

This tartlet, with a crisp mocha pastry and smooth Baileys mousse topped with ganache, makes a lovely dessert. A must if you like Baileys.

Equipment:	Scales, measuring spoons, bowl, saucepan, rolling pin, 7 x 7 cm (3 x 3") square or round tartlet rings, baking tray, greaseproof paper, baking beans, piping bags, No 1 tube, spatula, whisk, plastic bag.
Oven:	Pre-heat to 180°C, 170°C fan (350°F); Gas 4.

Mocha pastry		Group A
30g	Butter	• Rub the fat into the flour to form a crumble.
65g	Plain flour	

		Group B
30g	Caster sugar	• Place the coffee in a plastic bag and roll it flat.
5g	Cocoa powder	• Sieve the cocoa powder and coffee together.
4g	Instant coffee	• Add the cocoa powder, coffee, and caster sugar to the flour and fat crumble from Group A.
1	Egg yolk	• Bind together with the egg yolk.
		• Cover in cling film and rest in the fridge for 10 minutes.

Process

- Grease the tartlet rings.
- Roll out the pastry to 3mm thick and line the rings; chill for 10 minutes.
- Line the pastry cake with greaseproof paper and fill it with baking beans (See Hints and Tips for blind baking).
- Bake blind to set the pastry for about 10 minutes.
- Remove the beans and continue baking for another five minutes until the pastry is crisp.
- Allow this to go cold before Group C – filling with the mousse.

Chocolate Baileys mousse — Group C

100g	Milk chocolate couverture
50ml	Milk
20ml	Baileys
180ml	Double cream

- Place the milk in a saucepan and bring it to a boil; remove from the heat.
- Add the Baileys.
- Pour the milk/Baileys mixture onto the chocolate to melt it.
- Gently whisk until smooth; allow it to cool.
- Whisk the cream until it is at the soft peak stage.
- Gently fold the whisked cream into the chocolate until all of it has been incorporated.
- Place the mixture in a piping bag and pipe into the pastry case to ¾ full.
- Allow this to set.

Ganache — Group D

75ml	Double cream
8ml	Baileys
65g	Dark chocolate couverture
10g	Butter
½	Orange juice

- Place the cream in the saucepan and bring to a boil.
- Remove from the heat.
- Place the chocolate in a bowl and pour the cream on top of the chocolate; leave this for about 4 minutes to soften the chocolate.
- Gently whisk the chocolate and cream together to emulsify.
- Add the Baileys.
- Finally, add the butter and mix it into the chocolate.
- Place the ganache in a piping bag with a plain piping tube and pipe over the set mousse so that the ganache flows and creates a smooth top.

Topping — Group E

5g	Gold leaf
15g	Honeycomb pieces

- Place some of the left-over ganache into a piping bag with a No 1 tube. Pipe on the diagonal lines in one corner of the tart.
- Sprinkle some honeycomb sprinkles on top of the lines.
- Finish with a tiny piece of gold leaf.

- Grease the tartlet rings well to allow the pastry to release.

- Chill the pastry before baking, as this helps the pastry to relax and helps stop shrinkage.

- Baking blind is important. It only takes 10 minutes to make the case nice and crisp (See the section on Shortcrust and Sweet Pastry on page 33 for blind baking).

- Don't overwhip the cream for the mousse. It will have a bitty texture if overwhipped - this is where the fat globules pull together.

- Ensure you add the cream when the chocolate has chilled, otherwise, it will split.

- Mocha pastry helps develop the flavour.

Turkey Ham and Leek Pie

A delicious pie to mop up those Christmas leftovers in a lovely white wine sauce.

Equipment: Scales, measuring spoons, saucepan, spatula, sharp knife, chopping board, bowls, pie dish 23 x 17cm x 5cm deep (9 x 7 x 2" deep), pastry brush, rolling pin, star cutter.

Oven: Pre-heat to 200°C, 190°C fan (400°F); Gas 6.

Puff pastry		Group A
500g	Puff pastry	• See recipe and method in Autumn collection for Sausage, Bacon, and Mushroom Puff Pie on page 139 and 140.

Filling		Group B
300g (2 large)	Leeks	• Prepare the leeks by taking off the outside layer; cut off the end, and cut the leeks in half longways.
60g	Butter	
100g	Plain flour	• Rinse in cold water, ensuring there is no soil between the layers.
20g (1 tbsp)	Grain mustard	• Then cut into 3cm (1") pieces.
500ml	Hot chicken stock	• Place the leeks in a saucepan with a little water and cook to soften, then drain off the water.
150ml	White wine	
150ml	Crème fraiche	
500g	Cooked turkey meat	• Melt the butter and add the flour; stir in, and then slowly add the chicken stock and cook out for 5 minutes to ensure that there is no floury taste.
300g	Cooked ham	• Add the white wine, crème fraiche, and grain mustard.
Enough to season	Pepper	• Check the seasoning – you may need to add pepper.
		• Add the turkey, ham, and leek.
		• Place the filling into the pie dish, ready for finishing.

Topping	Group C

1	Egg	• Roll out the puff pastry from Group A to 5mm (⅛") thick.
20g	Plain flour	• Cut a thin strip to be placed around the edge of the pie dish; attach it with a little butter.
5g	Butter	• Egg wash the pastry strip and then place the pastry on top.

- Roll out the puff pastry from Group A to 5mm (⅛") thick.
- Cut a thin strip to be placed around the edge of the pie dish; attach it with a little butter.
- Egg wash the pastry strip and then place the pastry on top.
- Press down to attach and then trim the edges, so there is no overhang.
- Pinch the pastry to secure it. This also creates a design.
- Egg wash the pastry top.
- With any spare pastry, cut out some puff stars and place them on top to a design of your choice.
- Make sure there is a hole in the middle of the pie so the steam can be released during baking.
- Before baking, rest the pastry for about 15 minutes.
- Bake for 35 to 40 minutes.
- The pastry will lift and be crisp and golden when baked.

- This pie doesn't need to be made with just leftovers, of course.

- Detailed notes on puff pastry methods can be found in the Section on Puff Pastry on page 37.

- It could also be made with chicken – you just need to cook the chicken pieces first.

Apricot Jane's

Hints and Tips

- The ham could be exchanged with potato, which is best cut into cubes and cooked before adding to the sauce.

- Any leftover puff pastry could be made into cheese straws. Roll out the pastry to 5mm thick. Brush over with egg wash, then sprinkle parmesan cheese on top with a little sprinkling of paprika. Roll to attach the parmesan; turn the paste over and repeat, so both sides are covered in parmesan cheese and paprika. Cut into strips. Bake at 200°C, 190°C Fan (400°F).

Christmas Danish Mincemeat Cushions

I love Danish pastry, so I thought, instead of pastry mince pies, I would make Danish. I wanted the filling to be visible. Eat while slightly warm – ooh, so delicious.

Equipment: Scales, measuring spoons, large mixing bowl, spatula, zester, rolling pin, sharp knife, template for the Danish: 8cm (3") square, baking trays 30 x 20cm (12 x 8"), parchment paper, small saucepan, pastry brush, cling film.

Oven: Pre-heat to 190°C, 180°C fan (375°F); Gas 5.

Yield: 15 mincemeat cushions.

Preparation time: This recipe involves preparing the mincemeat a couple of days in advance.

Mincemeat — Group A

120g	Grated apple	• Wash the sultanas, raisins, and currants. Leave them to drain.
120g	Raisins	• In a large bowl, place all the ingredients and mix them together.
160g	Currants	• Then cover and leave for a couple of days.
120g	Chopped apricots	• This will benefit by being made in advance to allow the fruits to absorb the liquids and to plump up and mature.
60g	Mixed peel	• When ready to use, mix again to ensure the mix is nice and moist.
120g	Soft dark brown sugar	
30g	Ground almonds	
8g	Mixed spice	
1 zest and juice	Orange	
1 zest and juice	Lemon	
70g	Brandy	

Group B

120g	Suet (vegetarian suet can be used)	• When ready for use, add the suet and mix through the mixture.

Danish Pastry — Group C

250g	Strong flour	• Rub the butter into the flour.
15g	Butter	

Group D

25g	Caster sugar	• Add the sugar, salt, and dried yeast and mix together.
3g	Salt	• Make a well.
7g (1 sachet)	Dried yeast	• Pour the egg, cold water, and milk into the well and work in the dry ingredients to
65ml	Water (cold)	form a dough.
50ml	Milk	• Knead for 10 minutes to form a smooth elastic consistency.
1	Egg	• Allow to rest for 10 minutes.

Group E

200g	Butter	• Cut the butter into slices, ready to place in the dough.

Process for Danish Pastry

- Roll out the dough to a rectangle 30 x 15cm (12 x 6").
- Place the butter over ⅔rds of the dough. Then fold ⅓rd of the dough over ⅓rd of the butter. Then fold over the remaining ⅓rd of the dough (This is the same process as for the English method of puff pastry – see the Section on Puff Pastry on page 37).
- Roll out the dough again to the same measurements and fold in three. Wrap the dough in cling film and place it in the fridge for 15 minutes to allow the dough to recover (rest).
- Repeat the turn one more time; the dough will now have had three half turns.

Group F

1	Egg	• Mix the egg for egg wash.
30g	Grated marzipan	• The grated marzipan is part of the filling.

Process for the Mincemeat Cushions

- Roll the Danish pastry out to a 3mm thick rectangle. See the template at the back of the book.
- Using the 8cm square template and a sharp knife, cut out squares without dragging the pastry.
- Lightly brush the centre of each square with egg wash.
- Bring each corner into the centre of the square and press down.
- Lightly moisten with egg wash again and sprinkle about 2g (½tsp) of the grated marzipan on top.
- Place the mincemeat from Group A on each square – about a heaped teaspoon; press down gently.
- Allow the Danish to prove until double the size.
- Slightly press the mincemeat in place before baking.
- Bake for approximately 15 minutes until golden in colour.

Glaze   Group G

100g	Apricot jam	• Boil the apricot jam with a little water to thin it down for easy brushing.
1	Juice of lemon	• When you remove the cushions from the oven, brush them over with boiled apricot jam.
200g	Icing sugar	• Mix together the lemon juice and icing sugar to form the lemon icing. The consistency should be such that it can be lightly brushed over the apricot jam to complete the product.
		• Cool slightly before brushing over with the lemon icing.

- Make the mincemeat in advance, so it matures and has a good flavour.

- I grated some left-over marzipan - it definitely added to the flavour. It also adds moisture and texture.

- Apricot glaze helps to keep the product from drying out and gives it freshness.

- Lovely served warm.

- A nice change from pastry mince pies - give them a try!

- There is a template at the back of the book - see the Section on Templates on page 195.

Glossary

These are some words used that you may find helpful.

Aerate	To increase in volume.
Albumen	The name of the egg white.
Bake blind	Lining a flan with parchment paper and filling with beans, then baking helps to set the frame to eliminate soggy bottomed pastry tarts.
Batter	A smooth cake mixture.
Book turn	A type of fold-in puff pastry or Danish pastry making.
Bundt	A Bundt cake tin is ring-shaped with a hole in the middle to ensure the cake bakes evenly. Most Bundt tins have moulded swirly designs.
Bulb	A plain piped bold dome shape.
Butterfat	Refers to the amount of fat present in cream.
Caramelise	This is where the sugars change and give colour.
Cartouche	A paper lining to cover the pastry to protect it from the beans sticking to the paste. It can also be used as a cover in cooking.
Clear	To form a smooth mixture.
Coat	To cover a product.
Cob	A bold round ball shape.
Cook out	A term used to ensure that a mix, e.g., choux pastry, has been cooked well before the next stage.
Couverture	Chocolate that needs to be tempered for use.
Craquelin	A topping for choux that gives a crunchy textured top.
Cream	To mix together, e.g., butter and sugar, vigorously to incorporate air.
Crumb	The internal structure when the product is cut (cake and bread)
Crumble	A fine mixture of flour and fat.
Crust	The external surface of bread and cake.
Curdling	A separation of the liquid phase and fat phase of a cake batter.
Dariole moulds	A 6cm diameter small tin used for Madeleines or crème caramel.
Develop	A process of kneading to create the gluten network to form an elastic dough.

Divide	To cut the paste of dough into small units.
Dock	Making holes in the paste to reduce the lift in baking.
Dough	A mixture of flour and water where the gluten is developed.
Dropping consistency	A texture when the mix will drop from a spatula to form a V shape.
Dust	Distributing flour to prevent dough or pastry sticking or icing sugar for decorating.
Egg wash	Beaten egg used to glaze or secure paste. Can be a whole egg or yolk with a little water or milk.
Egg weight	The weight of the egg without the shell.
Enrich	The addition of butter, egg, milk, and sugar.
Elasticity	The dough will spring back to its original shape when handled.
Endosperm	The white starchy part of the grain.
Fermentation	The action of yeast in a dough.
Final proof	The last rise just before baking bread.
Finishing	The decoration of a product to complete.
Flash	To colour the surface quickly, could use a blow torch.
Foam	A light aerated mixture of sugar and egg for sponges or meringue.
Ganache	A mixture of boiled cream and chocolate used for coating or filling.
Garnish	Using extra materials to enhance the product for service.
Gelatinise	Where the starch cells open up on heating, creating a gel.
Glaze	To give the product a protective coating and attractive finish.
Gluten	Insoluble protein in wheat dough, formed from gliadin and glutenin proteins in flour.
Grease	Application of fat or oil on a surface to prevent the product from sticking.
Half turn	A type of fold-in puff pastry or Danish pastry.
Hoop	A frame used for baking.
Hydrate	To moisten dry ingredients.
Hygroscopic	To absorb moisture.
Incorporate	To combine and blend ingredients.
Intermediate proof	The stage between dividing and final moulding in bread.
Knock back	The process of lightly kneading bread dough during bulk fermentation to release the gas and strengthen the gluten network in preparation for dividing and shaping.
Lamination	Rolling dough and layering fat into the pastry to create layers.
Lift	Increase of volume during baking.
Mould	To shape the dough by working it.
	Microscopic organism related to fungi, i.e., mouldy.
Nibbed	When nuts are nibbed, it means they are chopped. Nib sugar is coarse sugar, which holds its shape when baked so it can be a dressing.
Oven spring	The increase of volume in the first stages of baking bread.
Paste	A blend of flour and fat, which, with liquid, forms a paste.

Pectin	A natural setting agent found in fruits.
Pin	To roll out.
Pipe	With the use of a piping bag, extrude the mix to create shape.
Polenta	Is ground maize, yellow in colour, no gluten.
Prove	The resting period to allow the dough to expand before baking.
Reconstitute	To hydrate dry ingredients for use.
Recover	A rest period to allow the gluten to relax.
Roux	A cooked mixture of fat and flour.
Savarin	A round mould with a hole in the middle.
Scrape down	To clear mixture from the sides of the bowl to ensure a well-incorporated batter.
Scraper	A plastic tool used to scrape bowls.
Scaling	To weigh out into smaller units.
Segment	A section – splitting into groups.
Short	A firm but tender eating quality.
Shortening	A 100% firm fat has no flavour and acts to shorten pastry or soften the crumb in cakes. Different brands are available, e.g., Trex, made from vegetable oil.
Silicone mat	Non-stick reusable mat for baking.
Skinning	The dough surface becomes dry.
Sweating	Moisture is trapped between the product and the tin/tray it has been baked in, causing the product to have wet patches, which could lead to mould growth.
Tempering	Working with liquids to certain temperatures for use. An important preparation step for couverture chocolate before use to achieve gloss and snap in the finished product.
Toughen	Overworked gluten development.
Tube	Comes in a range of shapes and sizes for piping.
Turntable	A rotating table used for decorating processes.
Volume	The depth of the baked product / the amount of mixture suitable for a tin.
Yield	The number of pieces from a mix.

Templates

Gingerbread Man

For the Gingerbread Men recipe on page 165 (see Winter Recipes), you will need to scale up the template below to approximately double the size. The final size for the recipe should be about 27 cm high. You can do this by hand or by scanning and using your computer.

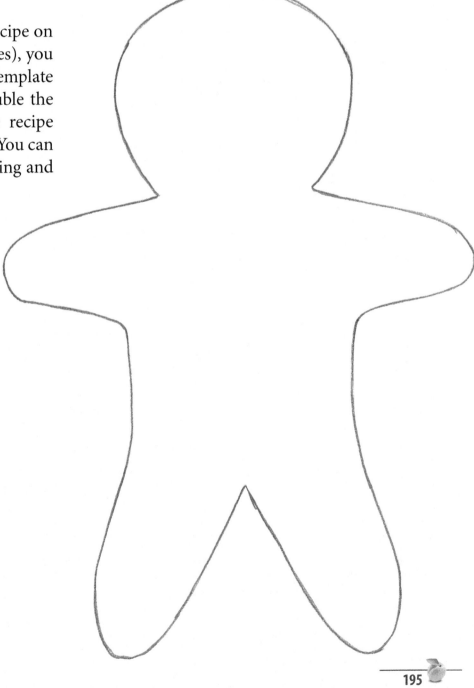

Heart Templates

These Heart templates are for the Shortbread Valentine Biscuits recipe (see Spring Recipes, on page 73). They are full-size and don't need scaling.

Danish Cushions

These two diagrams are for the Christmas Danish Mincemeat Cushions recipe (see Winter Recipes, on page 187). They show you how to fold the paste and are not to scale.

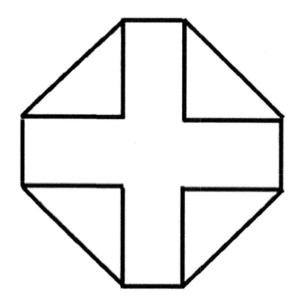

Acknowledgements

I have learned that one of the most important things in life is to say ***thank you***. By saying thank you, you are building up others, showing gratitude which gives value to those who receive it. I have been blessed with great friends and family who have believed in and encouraged me. They have been willing to try, test, and bake my recipes, give me feedback, and walk this journey with me, for without them, I couldn't do it.

So, a huge thank you to my husband Chris, who worked with me in taking the photos, a little different from his usual sports photography. We have had fun in this project together, and Chris got to test the products and is now a regular gym member!

Thank you to my baker volunteers, Sam Fynn, Caroline Chichester, Amy Adams, Fottiia Grivellis, James Mortimore, and Nikki Pink, who tested recipes at home for me and gave constructive feedback to me. Thank you to Chez Gawen and Chris Jeffcoate for checking over my written recipes and for welcome feedback. Thank you to Dr Devon Petrie and Sara Autton for checking my technical content.

Thank you to all my students who also kept asking me for a book – you spurred me on. I have learned so much over many years, so, armed with all this knowledge, I have finally put pen to paper.

Last but by no means least, a huge thank you to Philip Marsden, who has been a great source of encouragement in helping me with layout, grammar, and technical computer skills. Philip has kept me on my toes and challenged me along the way, for which I give you thanks; you have been instrumental in helping me bring it all together.

Partners

This book is produced in partnership with the industry I have loved and served for many years.

Thank you to:

The **Alliance for Bakery Students & Trainees'** aim is to promote and develop training through Colleges, Universities, and the Industry through courses, competitions, and workshops.

I served as Competition Secretary and President.

Cooplands was founded as a family firm. They now employ over 1,600 people and are the second-largest bakery chain in the UK.

I worked for Cooplands as a Bakery Trainer.

Worshipful Company of Bakers

The Bakers' Company can trace its origins back to 1155 and is the City of London's second oldest recorded guild. The Company's membership is drawn from those living and working in the City of London; from those working in the Baking Industry or Allied Trades.

I am proud to hold the Freedom of the City of London and to be a Liveryman of the Company.

The **Bakers and Confectioners Association**, established in 1905, consists of 60 elected Members who represent the Bakery Craft Sector throughout the UK and Ireland. Meeting regularly to promote the skills of the trade to a high standard and to exchange ideas to enhance their businesses.

As the voice of craft bakery since 1887, the **Craft Bakers Association** is passionate about the baking industry and keen to pass on knowledge and expertise for future generations.

Chris Hatton

Freelance Sports Photographer

chrishattonphoto@googlemail.com

Printed in Great Britain
by Amazon

15452503R00120